T0271416

Development as Swaraj

This book offers an in-depth insight into the Indian concept of Swaraj—self-rule—both in theory and practice and posits it within the larger context of development.

It opens by discussing the limitations of prevailing sustainable development paradigm as well as other heterodox development paradigms in achieving a sustainable and equitable future. Further, it constructs development theory around the idea of swaraj, based on the writings of MK Gandhi and JC Kumarappa. The swaraj development vision weaves in the morality of the greatest good of all, political decentralisation, and economic self-sufficiency as important elements to achieve an exploitation free social order that ensures more control for individuals over their lives. It reveals sustainability and equality as inherent features of such a non-violent social order.

The book then provides an introduction to the khadi—handspun and handwoven textile—sector, which is taken as a case study to demonstrate the swaraj development approach. The use of this sector helps readers to get a snapshot of the efforts that have been made since the time of Gandhi and Kumarappa towards the attainment of swaraj. Importantly, the khadi section highlights the method of translating theory into practice based on the unique three-pronged approach of the swaraj development paradigm. By showcasing how to establish swaraj within the khadi sector, the author offers insights into how it can be replicated for attaining a sustainable and equitable world.

The book will appeal to scholars and researchers in the fields of Gandhian studies and development studies.

Sumanas Koulagi is associated with Janapada Seva Trust, India. He holds a PhD degree in International Development from the School of Global Studies, University of Sussex, UK. He loves wildlife and is interested in development, an indispensable dynamic of present-day existence.

Routledge Studies in Development Economics

For more information about this series, please visit: www.routledge.com/Routledge-Studies-in-Development-Economics/book-series/SE0266

Development as Swaraj

Towards a Sustainable and Equitable Future

Sumanas Koulagi

LONDON AND NEW YORK

First published 2023
by Routledge
4 Park Square, Milton Park, Abingdon, Oxon OX14 4RN

and by Routledge
605 Third Avenue, New York, NY 10158

Routledge is an imprint of the Taylor & Francis Group, an informa business

© 2023 Sumanas Koulagi

British Library Cataloguing-in-Publication Data
A catalogue record for this book is available from the British Library

Library of Congress Cataloging-in-Publication Data
Names: Koulagi, Sumanas, author.
Title: Development as swaraj : towards a sustainable and equitable
future / Sumanas Koulagi.
Description: Abingdon, Oxon ; New York, NY : Routledge, 2023. |
Series: Routledge studies in development economics | Includes
bibliographical references and index.
Identifiers: LCCN 2022039374 (print) | LCCN 2022039375
(ebook) | ISBN 9781032404394 (hbk) | ISBN 9781032404400
(pbk) | ISBN 9781003353096 (ebk)
Subjects: LCSH: Sustainable development—India. | Economic
development—India.
Classification: LCC HC79.E5 K683 2023 (print) | LCC HC79.E5
(ebook) | DDC 338.954—dc23/eng/20221025
LC record available at https://lccn.loc.gov/2022039374
LC ebook record available at https://lccn.loc.gov/2022039375

ISBN: 978-1-032-40439-4 (hbk)
ISBN: 978-1-032-40440-0 (pbk)
ISBN: 978-1-003-35309-6 (ebk)

DOI: 10.4324/9781003353096

To everyone who has sustained and enriched me with their love, support, and sacrifice.

Contents

Figures

Praise

"It is clear in this climate-risked times, local communities must have control over their natural resources for livelihood security. I would argue that the new paradigm of development has to be rooted on the principle of self-rule. Sumanas's unique childhood background and academic work provides us important insights into the why and how this can be done. This is a must read."

—**Sunita Narain**, Centre for Science and Environment, Delhi

"This book very succinctly captures and brings back the central idea that was propagated by Gandhiji and Kumarappa to the fore. I strongly recommend the book as a stimulus for the development of an exploitation free social order, which is inherently sustainable and equitable."

—**Ela Gandhi**, Phoenix Settlement Trust, Gandhi Development Trust, and Religions for Peace International, South Africa.

"Very interesting and important topic."

—**Noam Chomsky**, MIT

"Sumanas offers a close, friendly and frank study of the concept of *Swaraj* and produced a pertinent reflection on development, the environment, and human dignity."

—**Rajmohan Gandhi**, author of biographies and histories, including *India After 1947* (2022)

"This book offers a courageous reinvigoration for today's crisis-ridden world. A refreshing vision of hope, written with inspiring clarity, that reasserts an indigenous Indian concept of development based on *Swaraj*."

—**Felix Padel**, Centre for World Environment History, University of Sussex

"In times of increasing global inequality, deteriorating democratic institutions and escalating climate catastrophe, Sumanas recovers vital insights from Gandhi and Kumrappa's conception of *Swaraj*, an alternative paradigm of development. This book offers us a vision of how to surmount the violence inherent in prevailing systems of moral political economy."

—**Earl Gammon**, Centre for Global Political Economy, University of Sussex

"*Development as Swaraj*, must be read as a corrective to the dominant development paradigm based on political centralisation and economic growth. One cannot contest Sumanas's argument for the critical need for the reassertion of a socio-political economic order, which couples progress with ethics."

—**Aruna Roy**, Social Activist, and member of Mazdoor Kisan Shakti Sangathan (MKSS)

"Ever since the National Planning Committee of 1938 sidelined the position represented in it by JC Kumarappa, Gandhian ideas about political economy receded into the background and were never given a serious run in India. In the small, but devoted, body of writing that still explores the great merit in those ideas, Sumanas Koulagi's new work is a very worthy addition. Drawing upon a scrutiny of the Khadi institutions in Karnataka, Koulagi presents an argument for integrating the notion of development with Gandhi's ideal of Swaraj, and deploys it skillfully to make fundamental criticisms of prevailing notions of development, including the seemingly well-intentioned ideas around the notion of 'sustainable' development. This is a very thoughtful book and a very necessary one."

—**Akeel Bilgrami**, Columbia University

"Important and brilliant subject."

—**Robert Chambers**, IDS, UK

"This book is a much-needed contribution towards the existing literature on swaraj and khadi. It is the combination of theory and practice that gives value to this account."

—**Uzramma**, Malkha, India

"*Swaraj* has resonance unequalled by any word in the Indian subcontinent. Sumanas Koulagi through insightful reading of Gandhi and J C Kumarappa has delved deep into the universe of Swaraj. His reading is deeply political and one that urges us to action. It is both a paean and a panacea to India."

—**Tridip Suhrud**, Professor and Provost CEPT University, Ahmedabad

"I endorse and would strongly recommend that young Indian citizens read and digest the pulsating heartbeat of Sumanas Koulagi's vital book, *Development as Swaraj* as a way of preventing the impending tragedy of intergenerational colonisation that threatens to over-whelm and erode the gains of India's non-violent Independence movement. Not surprisingly, the author accurately hones in on 'the gradual disappearance of wilderness' as a key factor that has brought us to a near-breakdown of India's ecological and social structures, without which any hope of peace would be a chimera."

—**Bittu Sahgal**, Sanctuary Asia

Preface

This book is a response to the sweeping changes that I have experienced over the years in three spheres of my life: family, society and environment. But before delving in detail into those transformations, let me begin with a brief autobiographical note.

I grew up on an organic farm near Melukote, a small town in South India. The farm was also the site of a family-run voluntary organisation called Janapada Seva Trust[1] that engages with a host of community issues such as livelihoods, education and environment. It was started in 1960 by my grandparents, Surendra Koulagi and Girija Koulagi, who came from a generation that was influenced by the aura and ideals of Mahatma Gandhi. Naturally then, this influence percolated into the life of my father and, through him, into mine. My parents' decision to not put me through a formal schooling made a big difference to my formative years. I was encouraged to participate in various activities of the organisation and was provided an opportunity to spend time with visiting scholars and activists from around the world. These interactions made me realise the interdependence of life. This, in turn, encouraged me to go beyond the limited realm of my family and care about the society and environment as well.

Now let's turn to the aforementioned sweeping changes. I believe this will help you understand the deeper truths that I seek to uncover in this book.

First of the three transformations was the result of unforeseen changes in my family. I always loved spending time with my grandparents. Their affection and care were unmatched. The way they transitioned from being mentors in my early days to friends and co-travellers as I grew up was intrinsically a phenomenal educative experience. From teaching me how to play chess to urging me to participate in passionate discussions on social and environmental issues, I shared a beautiful relationship with my grandparents. Similarly, I always cherished the encouragement that I received from my parents and uncle to explore all facets of life. However, the unexpected demise of my beloved grandparents and uncle shocked me into confronting the ephemerality of life.

The second transformation was brought about by a keen observation of the growing disparity in the living conditions of people in the larger social fabric. During my childhood, there were a dozen communities with their own specialised occupations living in Melukote. Each community had its own block in the town. There were weavers, carpenters, oil pressers, farmers, potters, bamboo workers, priests and so on. Walking through the narrow streets of Melukote and watching people engage in these various activities was a sheer joy. Although there were differences between the living conditions of different communities, life thrived. Each and every part of the town was distinctly vibrant in its own way. But over the course of time, the 'living spirit' of the town has eroded. Most of these occupations have now become economically unviable and the younger generation has moved to nearby cities in search of alternative livelihoods. Today, most blocks of the town have merely become a place for passing one's sunset years. The disparity between rural and urban spaces has reached its criticality.

The third transformation was caused by the gradual disappearance of wilderness that once flourished in and around Melukote. Over the years, many landscapes have been altered to create infrastructure projects. With the introduction of canals and borewells, traditional rain-fed farming has been turned into irrigated agriculture, dependent on chemical fertilisers and pesticides. Cash crops have completely replaced food crops once grown for subsistence. Millet fields that once fed flocks of munias, parakeets and herds of blackbucks have disappeared. Fig trees that were part of rain-fed agricultural system and host to innumerable wild creatures outside the forest are now despised and felled at the slightest of excuses. It is no surprise then that the chopping down of these huge fig trees is also metaphorically severing Melukote from its once abundantly diverse way of life. With the arrival of tap water, ponds, tanks and lakes that were once the lifeline of Melukote are slowly drying up and dying out of neglect. These sources of water, which were home to a variety of fish, frogs and birds are being encroached upon by construction activities. Old mud-houses that once sheltered the house sparrows are being slowly replaced by shiny concrete structures. In short, Melukote's rich interdependent life is on the verge of a breakdown, with the gradual loss of its essential wilderness.

These three transformations propelled me on a decade-long search for answers to the following questions:

a)   What is the purpose of this impermanent life?
b)   How to reduce disparity in society?
c)   How to conserve wilderness?

In my quest, I realised that all three questions are interconnected and the answer lays at the conception of development. It became evident that the purpose of life is largely moulded by the prevailing development paradigm. Development through accumulation of excessive material wealth has become the sole purpose of life. In a way, this notion of development has become the key factor that decides the degree of inequality present in the society and the level of impact that we leave on our environment. Therefore, I started looking for an appropriate development paradigm that could lend true purpose to life while reducing the disparity in society as well as the negative impact on environment.

In time, I realised the limitations of the prevailing sustainable development paradigms, which I have explained in detail in the opening chapter of this book. As a third-generation member in a Gandhian family, I had often wished to move away from Gandhi. However, the more I strove to do so, the better I started seeing the light in his thoughts and in that of his associate economic thinker, JC Kumarappa. Their central idea of *swaraj* or self-rule provided compelling answer to the purpose of life, and solutions to inequality and environmental crisis. Further, this chosen path led me to an MSc in Biodiversity, Conservation and Management at the University of Oxford and a PhD in International Development at the University of Sussex. In this book, I have tried to share the glimpses of all that I discovered in a decade-long quest. It is my firm belief that this book may provide you with some answers to the purpose of life while making of a sustainable and equitable future for all.

Note

1 More about Janapada Seva Trust can be found at www.janapada.org.

Acknowledgements

This book is a revised version of my PhD dissertation that was completed at the School of Global Studies, University of Sussex, UK. Therefore, first and foremost, thanks must go to my supervisors Dr Earl Gammon, Dr Vinita Damodaran and Professor Anke Schwittay. Their guidance throughout the various phases of this project has been invaluable. I have greatly benefitted from their constant encouragements and criticisms during these past several years. I also extend my sincere thanks to the examiners Professor Deepak Malghan and Professor Peter Newel, who made substantive and helpful comments on the original thesis.

Numerous people have helped me during this journey and mentioning their names here would not be sufficient to thank them. However, my gratefulness goes, in particular, to the khadi workers who generously allowed me into their world of work and lives. During the fieldwork, I was assisted by my friends Raghu GN, Kalleshi TJ, Suman CL and Shashank CL, without whose enthusiasm and support I would have missed out on a lot. I express my gratitude to Sachidananda KJ for helping me with illustrations that have been used in the book. I thank my friend Nalme Nachiyar for carefully proofreading my entire final draft.

I am grateful to Jamnalal Bajaj Foundation for their financial support without which it was impossible to complete my doctorate. I thank Jay Pullur of Pramati technologies, Guru of NR groups, BR Pai of Vijay foundation, and Dilnavaz Variava of Sidhwa Trust for their financial assistance. Also, I am thankful to Minal Bajaj, Dhirajlal Mehta, Ramachandra Pailoor, Hugo Dixon, Shrikanth Nonabur, Walter Peklo, Alistair Mackenzie, Swarup Anand, Anantha Sayanan, Janardhan CS, Alison Rector and Eric Rector for helping me out with funds whenever there was a need. It would not be an exaggeration to say that Sarah Kline and Ethan Kline were my lifeline outside the university. Without their generosity and encouragement, I would not have finished my doctoral program and, in turn, this book.

The support provided by my extended family has been an important source of sustenance. I thank Archana for her love, patience and understanding. I thank my parents Santosh and Geetha, siblings Supraj and Suhasini for their support, affection and love. My academic progress has been a direct product of their innumerable sacrifices. My biggest regret, as I write this, is that my grandparents Surendra and Girija as well as uncle Sughosh did not live to see me complete this book.

I would like to take this opportunity to thank Routledge for their prompt and helpful assistance with the manuscript at various stages of preparation. I am indebted to Kristina Abbotts and Christiana Mandizha for their enthusiastic encouragement. I am thankful to Bhaskar Kumar Kakati and Sanjeeb Kakoty for reading and giving excellent comments on the manuscript at the critical stage. Any inadequacies that remain, however, are my own.

Introduction

Each day dawns with multitudinous statements about this phenomenon called 'development.' It is worshipped by the modern world. Narendra Modi, the prime minister of India endorsed it in February 2021 when he said, 'development is our aim, development is our religion.'[1] This perception is not specific to India and has been the most important agenda of every single nation-state in the world. Development has become a 'global faith' and a central organising principle that defines global social order.[2]

So, what does development mean? Despite being a versatile term, development as a concept has 'a more coherent core of meaning which goes beyond its diverse substantive definitions.'[3[p.2]] It is essentially an intentional act, originating from an enduring human tendency to transform existing living conditions closer to the perceived notion of prosperity.[a] This essence of development has always been a key driving force in human history. In short, development not only lends purpose to our existence but also sets a direction for humanity.

The prevailing sustainable development paradigm has engendered inequality and environmental crisis that gravely threaten the collapse of human civilisation.[4–6] The growing inequality, particularly of wealth, has reached a point where the top 1% owns more than one-fourth of the total wealth shares.[7[p.9]] According to the latest World Inequality Report, if inequality is not adequately addressed, it may result in 'various sorts of political, economic, and social catastrophes.'[7[p.8]] At the same time, we are breaking through thresholds of delicately interconnected planetary boundaries, which delineate a 'safe operating space for humanity.'[8[p.32]] The growth of civilisation beyond these ecological limits will result in 'non-linear, abrupt environmental change,' and will have a fatal impact if not checked.[8[p.32]] Out of nine planetary boundaries, four have already been transgressed.[9] Therefore,

DOI: 10.4324/9781003353096-1

reducing inequality while keeping human civilisation within planetary boundaries is one of the most critical challenges facing humanity today. The key reason for the repeated failure of sustainable development to tackle burgeoning environmental crisis and inequality is the contradiction embedded in its notion of prosperity. Through critical observation of the sustainable development goals (SDGs), we can recognise prosperity defined in terms of possessing more material wealth while achieving distributional equity, and environmental sustainability.[10] However, there is a clear tension between the objective of wealth accumulation and the other two goals of equity and sustainability. If we try to achieve the former, the goals of equity and sustainability become suspect. Similarly, an overemphasis on the latter violates the former objective of augmenting fortune.

The root cause of this incoherence needs to be inquired with reference to well-known economist Amartya Sen's idea of development as freedom.[11] Sen's vision of development led to the formulation of the Human Development Index (HDI), which has significantly shaped the definition of prosperity in the sustainable development paradigm. That influence is evident in the following statement of the United Nations Development Programme (UNDP)

> there might be a case for using the HDI as one of a very few measures to summarise progress towards the 2030 Agenda... And if the HDI is moving in the right direction, it is rather likely that those SDGs are progressing too.[12]

According to Sen, freedom is the 'principle means' and 'primary ends' of development.[11] The objective is to increase 'substantive freedoms' like economic facilities, political freedom, social opportunities, protective security and transparent guarantees for 'people to lead the kind of lives they have reason to value and to enhance the real choices they have.'[11[pp.38,293]] Although it appears to be normatively well-anchored, the fundamental problem lies with Sen's conception of the individual, which is key to any development paradigm. The very idea of the individual is defined by her/his perceived relationship with other beings in the cosmos. It encompasses conceptions of right and obligation, where the former is about carrying out actions that one has reason to value and the latter entails one's responsibility towards other beings.

From Sen's point of view, obligation 'requires' a right in the form of freedom.[11[p.284]] In other words, a right is the source of obligation, where one's interest is placed over the interest of others. Such an understanding of the individual is grounded in conceptions of humanism that crystallised during the European Renaissance, particularly from a strand of thought that emphasised the importance of an individual's expression.[13] It was notably embodied in the emergence of the artist as a creator during this period. This humanistic tradition became the basis for later emergence of the liberal tradition in the enlightenment period of the 17th century. It conceived the individual as having 'possessive quality,' and also as the 'proprietor of his own person or capacities, owing nothing to society' making 'impossible' to 'derive a valid theory of obligation.'[14[pp.3,271]] This reflects in the right-based conception of an individual in Amartya Sen's idea of development. As right becomes the primary concern, care for others is disavowed. In other words, there is clear 'tension' between the notions of 'liberty and equality' having a 'zero-sum' relationship where increase in one is a proportionate decrease in the other.[15[p.126]] The result is the contradiction within the conceived notion of prosperity in the sustainable development paradigm, leading to contemporary problems of inequality and environmental crisis.

These growing problems have given rise to alternative conceptions of development. The heterodox approaches, though quite varied, are generally critical of the prosperity notion defined in terms of possessing more material wealth. Even though we can name numerous development paradigms for this approach, prominent among them are Buen Vivir from Latin America, Ubuntu from South Africa, Radical Ecological Democracy in India, the post-development tradition primarily from the United States, the degrowth movement in the Global North and the Gross National Happiness Project in Bhutan.

The Buen Vivir movement arose from the indigenous communities of Latin America during the end of the last century in reaction to development schemes based on economic growth. It is premised on a conception of a good life that encompasses living harmoniously with nature while respecting biological and social diversity.[16] It envisions a collective wellbeing of both human and non-human worlds.

Likewise, the conception of Ubuntu emerged in Zimbabwe and South Africa during their decolonial movements in the later part of the last century. It is based on the idea of mutual care rooted in certain African cultures. The conception is embedded in their popular proverb: 'a person is a person through other persons.'[17[p.52]] It is an understanding that the existence of an individual is inextricably linked with the lives of others and aspires for a cooperative society.[18[p.94]]

The Radical Ecological Democracy movement unfolded in India in 2012 out of grassroots initiatives. It envisions development as a bottom-up project based on participatory democracy with a recognition of the rights of non-human beings, as opposed to human-centred representative democracy.[19] It advocates for individuals' participation in key decisions that affect their lives in pursuit of a socially equitable and ecologically sensitive world.

The post-development approach came up in the 1980s in the United States as a response to the theories of development based on economic growth rooted in colonial development discourses. It questions the dominant discourse of development and calls for a world of pluralistic sensibilities or 'pluriverse of socio-natural worlds.'[20] It fundamentally challenges the prevailing notion of development that envisions the Global North as advanced and progressive and the Global South as backward, degenerate and primitive.

The conception of degrowth has its roots in the 19th century anti-industrial movement in the Global North. More contemporarily, it was popularised by André Gorz, a French philosopher in the 1970s. The conception questions economic growth while calling for downsizing of production and consumption to achieve sustainability and social justice.[21] It visualises a society based on cooperation, care and solidarity and advocates democratic decision-making and sufficiency in order to reduce consumption and waste.

The Gross National Happiness (GNH) is a philosophy that informs the government of Bhutan. It was promoted by Jigme Singye Wangchuck, the fourth king of Bhutan, in the early 1970s. It considers collective well-being as the marker of progress, the philosophy of which also forms the central tenet of the constitution of Bhutan that was enacted in 2008.[22] By recognising material and spiritual aspects of life as part of Gross National Happiness, it fundamentally challenges the concept of Gross Domestic Product (GDP), the prevailing benchmark of development.

Although these heterodox development paradigms try to tackle inequality and environmental crisis, they are limited in scope because the perception of wellbeing that is central to many of these approaches is inherently a 'subjective phenomenon.'[23[p.2]] This, in turn, poses a serious challenge to accommodating people with diverse outlooks, attitudes and cultures into the fold of their development models. Further limitation comes from their little emphasis on ways to overcome the exploitation imminent within their paradigms. This issue is appositely articulated by human geographer RN Vyas who says, 'close scrutiny shows that there are many dogmatisms and unsavoury features of class, gender, ethnicity, etc., hidden within these alternative models,' and that little attention has been given to the ways of overcoming those problems.[24[p.118]]

It is in this context that the Swaraj Development Paradigm becomes pertinent. The term swaraj is derived from the Sanskrit word *swarajya*, which originally means 'self-mastery' or 'self-control' aspired in order to attain 'freedom from desires.'[25[pp.429,434]] Among the different interpretations put forward by various nationalists and social reformers during the Indian freedom movement, the conceptualisation of swaraj as self-rule by Mohandas Karamchand Gandhi and Joseph Cornelius Kumarappa stands prominent. Gandhi led the Indian freedom movement of 'continental proportions,' and Kumarappa, a trained economic thinker from Columbia University, became one of his most important associates.[26,27] It is essential to consider both these figures while understanding the Swaraj Development Paradigm, as its political content was originally filled by Gandhi and economic content by Kumarappa.

The conception of swaraj was envisioned in the first half of the last century and it mounted a challenge to both materialist and positivist theories of development that had shaped the political economy debates of the time. Gandhi and Kumarappa also critiqued and laid bare the standard assumptions about the need for centralisation of power and economic efficiency that undergirded the dominant development models. In an India that was seeking to achieve industrial modernity rapidly, their positions were unattractive to many. This resulted in a long period of neglect of their ideas.

Of late, however, growing inequality and environmental crisis are generating a renewed interest among scholars in exploring their thoughts. For instance, Gandhi has been recognised as 'patron saint of the Indian environmental movement'[28[p.47]] and Kumarappa as 'founding father of green thought in India.'[29[p.5477]] Their contributions towards creating an equitable society through social justice have been equally acknowledged too.[30] However, their conception of the Swaraj Development Paradigm has received limited scholarly attention and is considered as a 'lesser-known alternative' that lost to 'the overarching and dominating capitalist and socialist paradigms.'[24[p.110]]

Although much has been written on the conception of swaraj by Gandhi and Kumarappa themselves, there still persists a lack of comprehensive development theory and praxis. Before embarking on an effort to construct such a development paradigm, it is essential to understand that they were not just theorists but men of action. There was a dialogue between theory and practice in their work. Their understanding of the living condition had come from a deep engagement with their impoverished compatriots over the course of several decades. Their thoughts represented the lived reality of people. The outstanding feature of their work is a consistency that connects theory and praxis. Since their lives were intertwined with India's freedom struggle, their readers were ordinary people outside the mainstream scholarship. This means that while their writings are scattered there remains an immense coherence. Therefore, the first part of this book uses their writings as a springboard for outlining the Swaraj Development Paradigm.

Even though the Swaraj Development Paradigm challenges prosperity in terms of material accumulation in a way not dissimilar to the aforementioned heterodox development approaches, it provides a comprehensive political-economic praxis in relation to moral philosophy that could, arguably, be operationalised at a global scale. The pathway deviates from other existing transdisciplinary and critical approaches rooted largely in the schism between idealism and materialism by recognising the dialectical workings of moral and material ties in shaping the living conditions. The objective of the Swaraj Development Paradigm is to achieve prosperity conceived in terms of peace, which involves external harmonious relationship with others as well as internal tranquillity of the mind. However, outer and inner dimensions of peace are considered as interconnected facets of prosperity. In other words, the central quest of the Swaraj Development Paradigm is to establish a non-violent social order where everybody can rule over themselves while protecting the self-rule of others. Such a non-exploitative society holds equity and sustainability as its inherent features.

The second part of this book demonstrates swaraj development in practice by taking Khadi, the handspun and handwoven textile sector in Karnataka as an example. It explores the pragmatic ways in which swaraj could be established within the Khadi sector. Further, it also shows feasibility of these pragmatic ways through Janapada Khadi initiative. The section demonstrates the method of translating theory into practice based on the unique three-pronged approach of swaraj development paradigm that has been discussed in the next chapter. Khadi is specifically chosen because of its historical connection with the conception of swaraj. Khadi was part and parcel of the swaraj project during the India's freedom movement because on one hand, it had the capacity to support livelihoods of a vast section of impoverished society while on the other, it had the ability to act as a 'commodity of resistance against the colonial exploitation.'[31[p.10]] This historical relationship helps us get an understanding of the efforts that have been made with respect to the swaraj development in practice since the time of Gandhi and Kumarappa. However, as independent India embarked on its Jawaharlal Nehru-led modernisation project, the Khadi sector became marginalised. Today, the overall production of Khadi is just 0.1% of the total cotton textile output in India, whereas the mill sector accounts for 4% of production, the handloom sector 12–13%, and the power loom sector 76%, respectively.[32] I hope the section acts as a compass for us to similarly align various other sectors more in line with the swaraj development paradigm. In short, the book seeks to contribute concepts, methods and empirical evidence that can help overcome the violence ingrained in the existing global social order and achieve world peace.

Notes

a Prosperity corresponds to the idea of good life or a certain opinion on how one should live one's life.

References

1 PTI. Development is our religion: PM Narendra Modi. *The Economic Times.* 2021 Feb 19.
2 Rist G. *The history of development: From Western origins to global faith.* 5th ed. London: Zed books; 2019.
3 Koponen J. Development: History and power of the concept. *Forum for Development Studies.* 2020;47(1): 1–21.
4 Harvey D. *Seventeen contradictions and the end of capitalism.* Oxford: Oxford University Press; 2014.
5 Motesharrei S, Rivas J, Kalnay E. Human and nature dynamics (HANDY): Modelling inequality and use of resources in the collapse or sustainability of societies. *Ecological Economics.* 2014;101(5):90–102.
6 Fromm E. *The Sane society.* London and New York: Routledge Classics; 1955.
7 Alvaredo F, Chancel L, Piketty T, Saez E, Zucman G. *World inequality report 2018.* Paris: World Inequality Lab; 2017.
8 Rockström J, Steffen W, Noone K, Persson A, Chapin FS, Lambin EF, et al. Planetary boundaries: Exploring the safe operating space for humanity. *Ecology and Society.* 2009;14(2):32.
9 Steffen W, Richardson K, Rockström J, Cornell SE, Fetzer I, Bennett EM, et al. Planetary Boundaries: Guiding human development on a changing planet. *Science.* 2015;348:1217.
10 Borowy I. *Sustainable development in Brundtland and beyond: How (not) to reconcile material wealth, environmental limits and just distribution. Environmental history in the making.* AG Switzerland: Springer; 2017.
11 Sen A. *Development as freedom.* Oxford: Oxford University Press; 1999.
12 Conceição P. Human development and the SDGs | Human Development Reports [Internet]. United Nations Development Programme. 2019 [cited 2020 Feb 15]. Available from: http://hdr.undp.org/en/content/human-development-and-sdgs
13 Connell WJ, editor. *Society and individual in Renaissance Florence.* Berkeley: University of California Press; 2002.
14 Macpherson CB, Crawford B. *The political theory of possessive individualism: Hobbes to Locke.* Oxford: Oxford University Press; 1964.
15 Bilgrami A. *Secularism, identity, and enchantment.* Cambridge, MA: Harvard University Press; 2014.
16 Gudynas E. Buen Vivir: Today's tomorrow. *Development.* 2011;54(4):441–7.

17   Ramose M. *African philosophy through Ubuntu.* Harare: Mond Publishers; 1999.
18   Eze MO. *Intellectual history in contemporary South Africa.* London: Palgrave Macmillan; 2010.
19   Kothari A. Radical ecological democracy: A path forward for India and beyond. *Development.* 2014;57(1). https://doi.org/10.1057/dev.2014.43.
20   Escobar A. Beyond development: Postdevelopment and transitions towards the pluriverse. *Revista de Antropología Social.* 2012;21(1):23–62.
21   Demaria F, Schneider F, Sekulova F, Martinez-Alier J. What is degrowth? From an activist slogan to a social movement. Environmental Values. 2013;22:191–215.
22   Royal Government of Bhutan. The Constitution of the Kingdom of Bhutan. 2008. ISBN 99936-754-0-7.
23   White MD. The problems with measuring and using happiness for policy purposes. *SSRN Journal* [Internet]. 2018 [cited 2020 Feb 15]; Available from: https://www.ssrn.com/abstract=3191385
24   Vyas RN. *Development discourse in India. Economic geography: Volume 2: Urbanization, industry, and development.* New Delhi: Oxford University Press; 2016.
25   Brown CM. Svarāj, the Indian ideal of freedom: A political or religious concept? *Religious Studies.* 1984;20(3):429–41.
26   Damodaran V. The British Raj, Gandhi and his practice of politics in India in the 1930s and 1940s. In: Harris M, Csaba L, Agnarsdottir A, editors. *Global encounters, European identities.* Pisa: Pisa University Press; 2010.
27   Govindu VM, Malghan D. *The web of freedom: J. C. Kumarappa and Gandhi's struggle for economic justice.* Oxford: Oxford University Press; 2016.
28   Guha R. Mahatma Gandhi and the environmental movement in India. *Capitalism Nature Socialism* [Internet]. 1995 Sep 1;6(3):47–61. Available from: https://doi.org/10.1080/10455759509358641
29   Govindu VM, Malghan D. Building a creative freedom: J.C. Kumarappa and his economic philosophy. *Economic and Political Weekly.* 2005;40(52):5477–85.
30   Redkar C. *Gandhian engagement with capital: Perspectives of J C Kumarappa.* Thousand Oaks, CA: SAGE Publications; 2019.
31   Ramagundam R. *Gandhi's Khadi: A history of contention and conciliation.* New Delhi: Orient Longman; 2008. 298 p.
32   Uzramma. By hand: The looms that can lead India. *Bhoomi Magazine.* 2013 Mar.

1 Swaraj Development Approach

The Swaraj Development Paradigm takes a distinct three-pronged approach to comprehend social order and its transformation. It recognises that the living condition is the outcome of the dialectical interaction between morality and materiality. By doing so, it synthesises idealism and materialism. Further, by acknowledging humans always perform material practices keeping a specific purpose in mind, the approach is constructed based on three categories of questions that are essential to define a development paradigm: the normative question of 'what should be'; the interpretive question of 'what is'; and the pragmatic question of 'what can be.' The historical element of 'what was' is implicit in all three categories, formulated in the form of folds as shown in Figure 1.1.

The metaphor of a fold serves as a means of explaining the swaraj development approach, expressing the distinct articulations or inflections that arise from a common fabric. The metaphor is also used by others, notably Gilles Deleuze, the 20th century radical philosopher, who considered it 'not merely as a philosophical concept, but as a practical means by which all manner of intersections between ideas and cultural and existential practices can be developed,

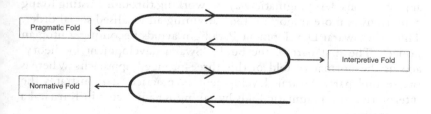

Figure 1.1 Visual representation of the Swaraj Development Approach.

DOI: 10.4324/9781003353096-2

maintained, and appreciated.'[1[p.9]] In this approach, the normative fold acts as the basis for the interpretive fold, which in turn fosters the pragmatic fold. The normative fold provides a definition of prosperity followed by a vision of the ideal social order. It offers 'a proper picture of what we want before we can have something approaching it,' even 'though never realisable in its completeness.'[2[p.136]] The interpretive fold involves an analysis of the existing living conditions by using the normative fold as a lens. The pragmatic fold concerns the future course of actions that can be taken based on the understanding of practical situatedness gathered from the interpretive fold to transform existing living conditions closer to the normative goal. The element of history persists across three folds because they are the result of past knowledge. The assessment of interpretive fold or the existing living condition against the normative fold acts as a foundation for the conception of development that accounts for the degree of transformation in the social order over time. In short, the three-pronged approach acts as a tool for translating swaraj development theory into practice.

Further, the Swaraj Development Paradigm escapes from the 'end of history' trap by taking this three-pronged approach.[3] It acknowledges the multiple ways of organising the social order and primarily challenges the disconnect between means and ends of human actions. It acknowledges the inseparable relationship between the two, like the indivisible connection between the seed and the tree. Moreover, the approach recognises that humans have 'control (and that too very limited) over the means, none over the end.'[4[p.237]] For example, one can decide to fly from Bengaluru to London but there is no absolute guarantee that one will reach the destination as intended. Anything can happen in-between. Therefore, it becomes important to carry out the actions with joy rather than thinking about the outcomes. Such a stress on the means encourages people to continue their work towards establishing a non-violent social order without becoming discouraged by the outcome of their efforts. In other words, this empathetic approach considers pragmatic ways of working through existing living conditions as more important than attaining an idealised social order. Thus, the Swaraj Development Paradigm avoids becoming a utopian project. The first part of the book, 'Swaraj development in theory' acts as the normative fold of this three-pronged approach. Whereas the second part, 'Swaraj development in practice' demonstrates the interpretive and pragmatic folds by taking Khadi sector in Karnataka as a case study.

References

1 Stivale CJ, editor. *Gilles Deleuze: Key concepts.* Ithaca, NY: McGill-Queen's University Press; 2005.

2 Gandhi MK. Independence. *Harijan.* 1946 July 28.

3 Fukuyama F. *The end of history and the last man.* New York: Free Press; 1992.

4 Gandhi MK. An appeal to the nation. *Young India.* 1924 Jul 17.

Part I

Swaraj Development in Theory

2 Swaraj Development Vision

This chapter explores the normative vision of the Swaraj Development Paradigm. By doing so, it represents the normative fold of the Swaraj Development Approach discussed in Chapter 1. The Swaraj Development Vision is built on a distinct framework called 'Moral Political Economy' (MPE). Aspects of this approach draw inspiration from the writings of 19th century polymath John Ruskin, in the case of Gandhi, and 20th century political economist Thorstein Veblen, in the case of Kumarappa.[1] By recognising the role of dialectical relationship between morality and materiality in shaping social order, and vice-versa, the MPE approach re-establishes a lost connection between moral philosophy and political economy. In doing so, it becomes a transdisciplinary approach. It is pre-disciplinary in its 'historical inspiration' and post-disciplinary in its 'current intellectual implications.'[2[p.89]]

The framework is pre-disciplinary in nature because 'moral philosophy consistently offered the most comprehensive discussion of human relations and institutions' before the emergence of social science disciplines in the later part of the 19th century.[3] The framework is also post-disciplinary in nature because of its capacity to work with emerging themes and problems that require transcending disciplinary 'boundaries to understand better the complex interconnections within and across the natural and social worlds.'[2[p.89]] In the MPE framework, morality represents the sense of right and wrong, politics denotes power relations and economy implies material relations. The three components are inseparably tied to each other like the various parts of a tree.

Natural Order

The Swaraj Development Vision is rooted in a cosmology of 'Natural Order' derived from the empirical understanding of material world in which humans are embedded.[4[p.46]] The development vision recognises

DOI: 10.4324/9781003353096-4

the impossibility of comprehending 'fully what is everlasting in the absolute sense' owing to the 'human intellect being limited.'[(5[p XI])] Within Time and Space in the Natural Order, there is nothing 'absolute'; rather it is 'relative' since 'everything begins somewhere and ceases to exist sometime.'[(5[p.X])] Nonetheless, human beings, as a part of the Natural Order, can comprehend a cosmic unity, where every being is interconnected through the chain of right and obligation. This 'Truth' of cosmic unity or interconnectedness of life becomes evident if we assess our everyday life.

Consider this: How does a cup of coffee that we drink in the morning become possible? There should exist a plant called coffee to start with, a honey bee or some insect must have pollinated its flowers to produce coffee fruits, someone should have harvested the seeds, someone else should have dried and powdered them, another person should have packed and sold the powder, yet another should have provided milk, and so on. Such collective contribution from so many unknown plants, animals and people across religion, caste, race, gender make our morning coffee a reality. Our existence is the direct result of the contributions made by others and this is true for every single thing we consume for our sustenance. Therefore, no being is superior or inferior and independent; everything works in relation to others as a part of a whole. An individual being in the Natural Order cannot become complete or achieve good outside of an association with others. Hence, any effort on the part of a being to dictate the Natural Order or disrespect the diversity results in self-destruction.

Just as the *Scala Naturae*, or the Great Chain of Being,[a] has been used in Western discourses of cosmology and ontology to justify God as Truth, the Swaraj Development Vision uses 'Truth is God' as the basis of Natural Order.[(7[p.264])] Human beings have a special place in cosmology because they are the only beings that are capable of comprehending the interdependence of life while possessing the capacity for free will—'the ability to either make or mar the orderly functioning of the Natural Order.'[(5[p.9])] By doing so, the development vision rejects the teleological notion of destiny. However, it recognises that the degree of human volition is determined by their moral and material conditions. Thereby, it fundamentally departs from *Scala Naturae* as well as the prevailing perception of human beings as 'self-defining subjects' possessing ultimate free will.[(8[p.374])] The development vision also undermines a key assumption of the Enlightenment, which is narrowly defined by an individualistic understanding of human nature. The vision considers human beings as creatures with both self-interest and selflessness.[(5[p.31])]

Such a binary nature of humans encompassing self-interest as well as selfless motivations is endorsed by recent studies, especially in the fields of neuroscience and psychology.[9–14]

The conception of the individual in the development vision is stipulated by self-rule that involves right and obligation. The right of an individual is about exercising one's will to express one's personality through 'creative faculties' and obligation is about the act of protecting self-rule of other beings in the Natural Order.[5[p.52]] Self-rule is not just concerned with rule over one's self but also with protecting the self-rule of others. Therefore, self-rule is a state of living where one effectively exercises one's right and obligation in the Natural Order.

The conception of self-rule is marked by an outer as well as an inner struggle. The outer struggle is a resistance to external oppression which is essential to exercise one's right. The inner struggle is the resistance to one's self-interest which is necessary to exercise one's obligation. Put simply, right is predicated on freedom from external constraints while the discharge of obligation is contingent on freedom from internal constraints. Hence, self-rule is not only an act against the oppressive forces embedded in social and state practices but also entails an internal struggle.

Since the existence of self is a direct result of the contributions made by others, one's survival involves not only an obligation to demand right but also a right to exercise one's obligation. In other words, obligation is the source of right. The inability to enforce one's right is nothing but the loss of freedom which is the result of collective failure of a society's political and economic structure. However, the failure to discharge one's obligation is always an individual failure. Indeed, a failure to fulfil one's obligation results in the negation of right. This obligation-based conception of the individual stands in contrast with the right-based conception of the sustainable development vision. It is critical to note that the vision of sustainable development is shaped by liberal and utilitarian traditions based on abstract sovereign (autonomous) rational individuals having no connection with others. The repercussion is inconsistency, accentuating a self-centred individualism that is indifferent to the cost projected onto others.[15[p.26]] The outcome is a breach in the chain of right and obligation in the Natural Order resulting in violence in the form of environmental crisis and inequality. This conception of individual, which gives precedence to obligation over right, forms the basis for constructing a morality of non-violence in Swaraj Development Vision.

Morality

Morality is the value on which individuals in a society operate, thus shaping the social order. As Kumarappa says, the 'most predominant value that prevails amongst people will colour a whole civilisation for centuries.'[5[p.40]] All moral values can be categorised into 'self-centric' and 'altruistic.'[5[p.31]] Self-centric values are rooted in relative truths and are subjective in nature. Here, 'things' are judged in 'relation' to oneself.[5[p.32]] A society based on self-centric values degenerates because of the clash of subjective interests; this results in violence and, in turn, self-destruction. Whereas altruistic values are 'objective' in nature and rooted in the absolute Truth of cosmic unity.[5[p.37]] Consequently, in the absence of a clash between subjective interests, society thrives.

Hence, the ultimate reality of existence is Truth and the means to live in such a reality is non-violence. Put differently, Truth is the teleological objective and one conforms to this cardinal moral principle to the extent that one practices non-violence in all aspects of their life. Although both Truth and non-violence are connected like the seed and the tree, means becomes more important than the ends.[16[p.67]] This is because human beings have 'control (and that too very limited) over means, none over the end.'[17[p.237]] For example, we can plan to grow tomatoes at our farm expecting some return. However, there is no guarantee that the crop can be grown as planned for we may fail to mobilise the required funds on time, face labour shortage, suffer from water scarcity, encounter an unexpected health crisis or be deterred by some other obstacle. Even if we succeed in growing tomatoes as intended, there is no assurance that we will get the expected return. The crop could fail due to a disease or pest attack or the yield could reduce significantly because of poor quality seeds or extreme weather events. Therefore, the development vision encourages individuals to perform actions without expecting returns since the outcome is essentially dependent on factors that cannot be fully comprehended and controlled by human beings.

Further, the Swaraj Development Vision defines non-violence in an active sense of love, which involves protecting the self-rule of others while defending one's self-rule from external domination. Such a conception of love encompasses qualities of selflessness and fearlessness, where the former entails a renunciation of self-interest and the latter is understood as the courage to defend oneself from external impositions. Both qualities are considered essential because selflessness helps an individual to exercise her or his obligation whereas fearlessness helps to exercise his or her right in the Natural Order. Thus, the morality of non-violence is rooted in the notion of the 'greatest good of all,' where 'all' includes non-human beings as well.[18[p.432],19] According to this moral stand, if one exploits the others, it is nothing but self-hindrance due to the underlying cosmic unity in the Natural Order. Therefore, individual good is inseparable from the good of all and a person is even expected to die for its realisation. It is here that the development vision departs from the sustainable development vision rooted in utilitarian and liberal traditions. However, non-violence is recognised as a process of reducing violence because it is constituent of the existence itself as described below:

> Strictly speaking, no activity and no industry is possible without a certain amount of violence, no matter how little. Even the very process of living is impossible without a certain amount of violence. What we have to do is to minimise it to the greatest extent possible. Indeed, the very word non-violence, a negative word, means that it is an effort to abandon the violence that is inevitable in life.[20[p.271]]

By considering human beings as a part of the cosmic unity, the development vision rejects all sorts of hierarchies and discriminations that occur because of differences in religion, gender, caste, class and sexuality. In short, the morality of non-violence is expected to act as a compass for individuals as well as collectives to follow.

Development and Prosperity

The conception of development in the Swaraj Development Vision is inherently tied to the notion of self-rule. The degree to which individuals respect their obligation as well as exercise their right reflects the degree of development.[4[p.28]] The development vision constructs a taxonomy of development by taking metaphorical examples from Nature. Human societies can be 'classified' into five different categories based on the degree of development.[5[pp.5–8]]

The first category is the 'parasitic' society, which rests fully on right and the complete disregard of obligation. The key feature of this society is 'self-love and pleasure seeking by the easiest route.'[5[p.55]] Individuals in such a society live on the exploitation of others to the extent of extermination. They do not exercise their creative faculties but live off the 'creation of others.' In other words, the personality of the individual is just an imitation of others because their exercise of creative faculties is insignificant. This group is noted as the 'house of imitation.'[5[pp.5–8]]

The second category is the 'predatory' society. Here too, individuals do not recognise obligation and sustain themselves by exploiting others but not to the extent of extermination. Individuals exercise their creative faculties to 'adopt' the 'creation of others' but still not 'enough to lay claim on originality.'[5[p.55]] In other words, people have the 'will-power to pick and choose but lack the sense of perspective to create anything complete and whole.' The individual personality is marked by appropriation of others' creation. This society is called the 'house of adoption.'[5[p.57]]

The third category is the society of 'enterprise' where there is a recognition of obligation only to those who support one's self-interest. The tolerance among individuals for different opinions is negligible, and there is a constant urge to force dissidents not to exercise their rights. Here, even though individuals exercise their creative faculties, they use it for their own benefit. This group is identified as the 'house of material creation.'[5[p.61]]

The fourth category is the society of 'gregation,' in which '[individuals] do not work for their own respective individual gains but for the common benefit of the whole colony like honeybees.' It represents 'an extension from self-interest to group-interest and from acting on immediate urge of present needs to planning for future requirements.'[5[pp.6–7]] At this stage, the '[individual] becomes more and more conscious that no one lives unto himself but that there are certain ties that bind [humans].'[4[p.26]]

Such a society can be sub-categorised into 'pack type' and 'herd type' based on their motives.[4[p.4]] Individuals 'unite for aggression' and their nature is 'predatory' in the pack type, whereas individuals 'gather together for safety' in 'herd type.'[4[p.3,4]] These motives define the nature of a group. This conception can be extended to human society, too. In the pack type, in spite of the shift in interest from individual to the group, society is still vulnerable to violence because the self-interest that is morphed into the form of group interest is hostile to outsiders. A society based on herd type motive is more peaceful within the group as well as towards outsiders. In such a society, individuals exercise their creative faculties towards the good of the society in which they are embedded. This sect is referred to as the 'house of social innovation.'[5[p.57]]

The fifth category is the society of 'service,' which is organised based on the full recognition of obligation that leads 'to an evaluation of each life in terms of others.'[5[p.7]] Individuals exercise their creative faculties for the benefit of others without expecting rewards. This results in a non-violent social order devoid of exploitation and becomes a society of 'permanence' that ensures peace. Here, the term permanence is 'relative' since the cosmology of Natural Order recognises that humans comprehend the world within Time and Space, where 'everything begins somewhere and ceases to exist somewhere.'[5[p.x]] Any society which fails to recognise the pre-eminent role of obligation leads to a society that is 'transient' or short-lived.[5[p.27]] Hence, obligation takes axiological precedence over right in the society of service. In such a society, individuals exercise their creative faculties and employ them selflessly for the good of all to become a 'house of sublimation.'[5[p.73]] However, the development vision recognises and describes the psychological and sociological foundations to construct a society strictly on obligation below:

> While it may be granted that group activity has a contribution to make within a limited community, it is open to serious doubt whether such activity is possible on a national scale for any length of time. A few idealists may get together and run an Ashram or other philanthropic institutions on the basis of service but whether such principles can be applied in the present stage of varied and varying civilizations on a world basis may be questioned... Experiments may be carried on under controlled circumstances in order to find out the laws that govern [socio-] economic movements but it is too much to expect humanity, as a whole, to function in like manner under normal conditions without such a controlled environment.[4[p.14]]

Nevertheless, the development vision aspires to the ideal of a society of permanence even if it is seldom attained in practice. It is considered as a direction for humanity to follow. The ultimate aim of life is to align one's self with the Truth.[4[p.31]] Therefore, the conception of development in the Swaraj Development Vision is as follows:

> Progress [development] signifies both the search after knowledge and truth as found in nature and its application to satisfy human needs. In the measure in which we are able to pull alongside nature's dictates, we shall be progressing in the right direction. But in so far as we are pulling against the course of nature, we shall be creating violence and destruction which may take the form of social conflicts, personal ill-health and the spread of anti-social feelings, such as, hatred, suspicion and fear. From these symptoms we shall know whether we are progressing scientifically or not. If our course of action leads to goodwill, peace and contentment, we shall be on the side of progress, however little the material attainments may be; and

if it ends in dissatisfaction and conflict, we shall be retrogressing, however much in abundance we may possess material things.[21[p.2]]

The conception of development shifts from the material plane to a spiritual or moral plane once basic material needs are fulfilled because human beings cannot operate on their moral self as long as they are materially destitute. In other words, '[a] starving man thinks first of satisfying his hunger before anything else.'[22[p.105]] Development is considered as a process of moving beyond the idea that we are separate selves by recognising the inter-connectedness of life. Such a process involves constant resistance to internal self-interest as well as external domination. The former involves the act of renouncing one's identity created by the egoistic self and the latter involves the act of renouncing the impression of one's identity that resides in others. In short, the Swaraj Development Vision aspires for an 'unalienated life' that ensures lasting peace.'[23[p.129]] Such an unalienated life demands individuals to exercise their 'liberty from the view of a more collective orientation to the world, i.e., from the point of view of the interests and concerns of all, is bound to *internally* cohere with equality in its outcomes.'[23[p.173]] Therefore, equality is not an '*extra*' but rather an 'outcome *built into* the deliverances of the exercise of the liberty.'[23[p.173]] By doing so, the swaraj development paradigm removes the long-standing tension between liberty and equality possessing a zero-sum relationship.

The Swaraj Development Vision contests predominant conceptions of prosperity in terms of 'high' and 'low' standards of living. In reality, the notion of high is nothing but a 'complex material standard of living' and low is a 'simple material standard of living.'[5[p.78]] The aspiration for a complex standard of living is the result of a 'multiplicity of wants' caused by the domination of self-interest over the moral self. Thus, it leads to a breach in the chain of right and obligation in the Natural Order, which in turn produces violence.

In contrast, the development vision of swaraj considers prosperity in terms of 'peace,' the innate outcome of self-rule and a non-violent social order.[24[p.150]] The conception of peace has inner and outer dimensions, where the former is a tranquil state of mind and the latter is a harmonious relationship of the individual with other beings in the Natural Order. These two dimensions of peace are considered inseparable as philosopher M Yamunacharya states, 'the quest for peace within one's own inner being and quest for peace or harmony in the external world are supposed to be the inner and outer sides of one and the same process of good living.'[25[p.2]] The result is a social order free of exploitation that is inherently equitable and sustainable.

Politics

The politics in the Swaraj Development Vision is aimed at creating power relations that enable individuals to self-rule. Therefore, it embraces a 'non-violent democracy' based on decentralisation of power.[26] A non-violent democracy advocates decision-making based on consensus where 'the decisions are not majority decisions but are made unanimous by winning over the dissenting minority.'[4[p.199]] The emphasis is on consensus precisely because it is the only way to ensure equal opportunity for everyone to actively participate in making decisions that affects their lives. In other words, consensus-based decision-making process guarantees that everyone's voice is heard irrespective of their backgrounds such as gender, age, caste, religion and class in decisions that are made. This in turn provides more control for individuals over their lives. By doing so, non-violent democracy deviates from the prevailing liberal democracy based on majoritarian decision-making process, which is inherently indifferent to minorities. However, it recognises the inability of humans to reach consensus effectively if individuals do not 'know one another at least by sight.'[27[p.140]] This is because, knowing helps individuals to empathise, which is essential for reaching consensus.[27[p.359]] Hence, participatory community that enables individuals to understand one another forms the basic unit of the non-violent democracy. Such a participatory community is expected to possess legislative, executive and judiciary powers and be 'self-sustain[ed] and capable of managing its affairs even to the extent of defending itself against the whole world.'[28[p.236]]b

In a non-violent democracy, the representatives are elected based on consensus from the participatory community to form governing bodies with an optimum scale that facilitate consensual decision making. Elected representatives at the lower-level governing bodies elect their representatives for the necessary higher-level governing bodies. The individuals, participatory community and any higher-level governing bodies are connected in the form of 'oceanic circles,' in which 'life will not be a pyramid with the apex sustained by the bottom,' but rather 'ever-widening, never-ascending circles.'[28[p.236]] In such a political system, 'the outermost circumference will not wield power to crush the inner circle but will give strength to all those within, and derive its own strength from it.'[28[p.236]]

Importantly, a non-violent democracy is constructed based on obligation where love acts as the central operating force, encouraging tolerance in individuals towards those who hold differences of opinion. In such a democracy, individuals are expected to refrain from interference into the lives of others, not because of hatred or indifference towards them, but out of love. Put differently, individuals are bound in a 'relationship of lasting affection' and tolerate others by recognising them as the 'translation of our own selves.'[31[p.36]]

By giving preference to obligation over right, non-violent democracy departs from the prevailing forms of democracies that discourage individuals from showing concern towards others by giving precedence to individual right. Further, the development vision recognises everyone, and not just elected individuals, as a political agent because every action of an individual continually affects the power relations in a society. Therefore, non-violent democracy is 'a living union between the government and the people.'[32] Since individuals are political agents, the state is not an end in itself 'but one of the means of enabling people to better their condition in every department of life.'[33[p.162]] The state is expected to ensure the self-rule of everyone and not interfere in the faith of individuals as long as they do not harm the faith of others.[34[p.63]]

The Swaraj Development Vision recommends the control of supply and demand by the state to ensure equilibrium in the production and consumption of goods. Production is expected to be regulated by 'licensing' and consumption by 'rationing.'[35[p.58]] Where feasible, the collection of tax by the state should be in the form of labour instead of capital. This is because the larger section of society has more or less equal access to the former than the latter. This, in turn, provides a fairer opportunity for individuals to fulfil their dues. However, by recognising the impossibility of excluding money in the contemporary world, it advises tax collection 'in kind' as far as possible.[4[p.149]] Further, it demands the collected tax to be spent 'as near the place of collection as possible' or 'within the catchment area of taxation' to 'increase the taxable capacity of the citizens.'[4[pp.149–50]] The people employed in the state machinery are expected to be paid the same as the 'average earnings of the citizens' and allowances should be paid 'partly in kind,' whenever possible, to prevent the exploitation of their positions.[4[p.145,149]]

Since all forms of institutions, including the state, are composed of individuals who are incapable of following the morality of non-violence in every possible circumstance, these bodies can often fail to protect the self-rule of individuals. Therefore, the development vision advocates *satyagraha* (insistence on Truth) as a necessary part of the political decentralisation process. *Satyagraha* is a non-violent method of conflict resolution. It is based on the understanding of the individual as an active political agent. Any kind of domination present in a society is not only the result of the actions of the oppressor but also of the oppressed. It is the cooperation between the two is the cause for any oppressive condition. In other words, the degree of toleration and acceptance of exploitation by individuals determines the level of violence present in a society.[16[pp.30–3]] Hence, it becomes an obligation for the oppressed to not to cooperate with a social order when it breaches their self-rule, and to change the situation through *satyagraha*.

The concept of *satyagraha* involves internal and external dimensions. The internal dimension encompasses an individual's resistance to one's self-interest. It is recognised that such an internal resistance requires self-knowledge and an understanding of Truth. This awareness encourages individuals to continually hold on to the Truth of interconnectedness of life and attain a state of selflessness, where one can perform actions without expectations in return. Such a state of mind helps one to operate according to the moral law of non-violence. The external dimension of *satyagraha*, on the other hand, involves resistance to oppression. Conflict arises in a society when individuals fail to act according to their moral selves, and when two parties hold contradicting opinions. Since relative truths are subjective and change over time, the first dimension of *satyagraha* is essential for a non-violent way of conflict resolution in society. It diminishes anger and hatred while encouraging the individual to see oneself in their opponent. In doing so, the love, the reflection of the Truth, becomes a medium of conflict resolution. It enables one to find mutuality with the opponent and transforms hate into voluntary 'suffering.'[16[p.75]] This, in turn, becomes an appeal to the moral self of the opponent and creates a path to consensus as described below:

> Our motto must ever be conversion by gentle persuasion and a constant appeal to the head and heart. We must, therefore, be ever courteous and patient with those who do not see eye to eye with us.[36[p.306]]

However, the development vision recognises that the means are more important than the ends because one has control over the former but not the latter. One becomes impatient and tramples on others' self-rule when the focus is on ends. Emphasis on means, though, encourages one to explore every opportunity to pursue dialogue with an opponent to reach an agreement. The openness to dialogue is central to *satyagraha*, since it lays the foundation for trust in the future:

> They say 'means are after all means.' I would say 'means are after all everything'... There is no wall of separation between means and

end... Realisation of the goal is in exact proportion to that of the means. This is a proposition that admits of no exception.[17[pp.236-7]]

The act of *satyagraha* involves different phases. First is the negotiation phase, where all the available channels are explored to reach an agreement with the opponent. If that does not work, then the second phase involves rousing public 'consciousness or conscience' through various media and offering a constructive solution.[37[p.22]] The third phase is 'self-immolation' through voluntary suffering and constant appeal to the opponent for agreement.[37[p.22]] Throughout the process, the disagreement is always with the opponent's action and not with the opponent, because individuals can change their disposition at any point in time. The process of resistance discourages individuals from criticising their opponent in any circumstance as it breeds hostility and departs from the path of non-violence. Instead, non-violence demands suffering, 'even unto death,' in the process of appealing to the moral self of the opponent.[38[p.69]] Such an act is undertaken to challenge indifferences and express readiness to hear the opponent's concern in a fresh way. As Gandhi articulated, 'things of fundamental importance to the people are not secured by reason alone but have to be purchased with their suffering.'[39[p.341]] *Satyagraha* acknowledges the defining role of emotions 'in consciousness and omnipresence in social behaviour'[40[p.1]], and thereby, in conflict resolution as well.

However, under exceptional circumstances, a violent act can become the reflection of a non-violent resistance. First, a violent act is sanctioned when the opponent seems to be unresponsive and damage by inaction is immediate and irreversible.[41[p.385]] The underlying intention of the act is of one's defence and not of rage, revenge or possession. Second, a violent action is endorsed when a being is 'suffering' without consciousness and 'recovery is out of the question.'[42[p.330]] The intention here not of self-interest but of relieving agony. These exceptions do not make the method of non-violent resistance open to scepticism, but reflect an 'ordinary' person's inability to conceptualise non-violent alternatives in every possible real-world situation.[41[p.385]] As a result, *satyagraha* becomes the non-violent way of challenging domination in society while establishing a harmonious social order.

Economy

The objective of economy in the Swaraj Development Vision is to meet the 'needs of people' within the 'restrictions under which nature has placed' them.[24[p.150]] It also considers every material transaction as a 'moral' transaction because the former has an irreversible sociological and environmental impact.[4[p.72]] The key concern of economy is to create an atmosphere where everyone can fulfil their basic material needs, which is a prerequisite for self-rule. Otherwise, people encounter the issue of survival, which is the primary source of self-interest and violence. Hence, self-rule embraces 'self-sufficiency' in the economy where individuals fulfil their essential material needs such as 'balanced food' that 'supplies the body with all its requirement in their correct proportions as to keep it fit and healthy,' in addition to 'adequate clothing and sufficient shelter.'[24[p.103,137]]

However, the development vision recognises the inability of individuals to obtain all material necessities by themselves. Therefore, it defines self-sufficiency as a 'relative term,' whereby the tendency is towards reducing the distance between production and consumption to a 'minimum.'[24[p.103]] Further, it identifies the chances of disproportionate share of material accumulation among individuals in the society, as everyone is endowed with different capacities and capabilities to participate in the economy. Therefore, individuals are expected to operate on the basis of 'trusteeship,' where any material abundance more than one's need is used for the welfare of others.[43[p.21]] By doing so, it ensures the morality of the greatest good for all.

The key feature of self-sufficiency is its emphasis on 'human personality' that enables individuals to 'make the higher life' possible.[24[p.103]] The human personality is defined by the degree to which one follows the moral code of non-violence while exercising one's intellect and talent. The development vision considers self-sufficiency as an organising economic principle for the entire society, which encompasses the production, exchange, consumption and disposal of goods. By regarding it as an organising principle, the development vision goes beyond the narrow notion of self-sufficiency in terms of individual self-help as conceived by Seymour, the chief proponent of self-sufficiency in the last century.[44] Further, by giving intrinsic value to self-sufficiency, the development vision departs from the definition of ecological economist Thomas Princen, a prominent contemporary advocate of sufficiency, based on the notion of 'enough' as an inevitable reaction to the environmental crisis.[45]

By focusing on human personality, the Swaraj Development Vision deviates from the modern forms of economic system which are centred around material creation and utility maximisation.[24[p.103]] Further, it challenges the fundamental notion of efficiency, which is the vital driving force behind the prevailing economic systems. It is essential to understand the origin of the concept of efficiency and its impact on society to appreciate self-sufficiency in its fullest sense. Efficiency, as an idea, first emerged in the field of mechanics, particularly in the context of efforts made to enhance the productivity of waterwheels in the mid-18th century.[46[pp.1–75]] The concept was later applied to human societies through social Darwinism coupled with Taylorism[c] in the late 19th and early 20th centuries, making economic efficiency central to the project of modernity. The implication of this is an increased control over production and associated social relations in the contemporary global social order by a small section of people, resulting in a centralisation of political power.[46[pp.148–61]] The tendency of an economy based on efficiency is one of 'control' and exploitation.[46[p.xiv]] Thus, an economy focused on efficiency leads to competition, domination and violence, whereas self-sufficiency encourages cooperation, self-rule and peace.

Economy in human societies can be categorised based on its use of two fundamental kinds of material flows available in the Natural Order. One type is the 'reservoir economy,' which is built on resources that are limited or exhaustible. The other is 'current economy,' which is constructed on resources that 'can be increased by man's effort or are inexhaustible.'[4[p.25]] A society based on reservoir economy is predatory in nature because it draws on resources which it has not contributed to in any manner. It breaks the chain of right and obligation in the Natural Order, resulting in violence. In contrast, a current economy fulfils the right and obligation chain of Natural Order and leads to a non-violent society. Consequently, the economy of self-sufficiency embraces renewable resources over non-renewable resources as the basis of its material flow.

The nature of production defines the structure of social order. The development vision recognises production as a primary component of the economy that shapes human personality. Since the conception of work is central to the production component of any economy, the development vision constructs this idea based on the 'cycle of life' present within the Natural Order.[5[p.2]] The work carried out by all sentient beings to fulfil their material needs has two elements. One is the 'creative element' that helps improve their skills to fulfil material needs in a constantly evolving ecological setting. The other is 'toil' or 'drudgery' in the form of repetitive action which is necessary for perfection and satisfying material needs.[47[p.2]] Both the elements make 'wholesome' work to maintain the continuous cycle of life in the Natural Order.[47[p.2]]

A balance between creativity and drudgery is essential for self-rule. Without this, the former becomes 'indulgence,' where the individual cannot discharge obligation, and the latter becomes a 'drag' or devoid of 'interest,' where individuals cannot discharge right due to the lack of space for exercising their creative faculties.[4[p.62],47[pp.8,17]] Since both conditions are inimical to self-rule, any separation between the two becomes a fundamental source of violence and diffuses throughout society. Therefore, any tendency in individuals to retain the creative component of work, that which is 'playful,' while displacing the toil component onto others leads to the degeneration of society. The manifestation of this separation is evident in the stark division of labour seen in contemporary global society. For example, the extreme division of labour present in the garment industry has resulted in exploitation where '[t]he workers are disposable, rags of humanity, as it were, used up like any other raw material in the cause of production for export.'[48[p.3]]

The conception of wholesome work is about the 'function of work' rather than the 'product' of work.[5[p.107]] Wholesome work is the 'means of developing one's personality in all three aspects of intelligence, character and artistic sense,' along with fulfilling material needs that enable individuals to act from their moral self.[47[p.9]] The division of labour in wholesome work provides 'diversion and variety in sufficient measure in every sub-divided unit of it to prevent it becoming a stain on the nerves.'[47[pp.12–13]] Further, it ensures 'full scope' for all the physical and mental 'faculties' of the workers, permitting them to 'comprehend the full implications of their activity' while producing articles that are in the form of 'complete marketable units.'[47[p.17]] In consequence, the development vision of swaraj departs from the modern form of division of labour, which is based on efficiency in material production.

Similar to division of labour, leisure is another crucial component of wholesome work. Again, the relationship between work and leisure is derived from the Natural Order. Work and leisure are tied to each other in the cycle of life. Imbalance in these two components breaks the cycle, resulting in violence. The work part becomes drudgery and the leisure part becomes indulgence, both of which are inimical to self-rule. Thus, wholesome work does not disaggregate work and leisure into separate spheres, as described here:

> Leisure is an integral part of work just as rest is an essential component of a musical note. The two cannot be taken apart. Leisure is not a complete cessation of all activities. That will be death. Neither is leisure idle time. Idleness leads to deterioration. Beneficial leisure provides rest to one faculty, while other parts of our personality are being exercised. A mental worker at his desk needs an active hobby like gardening to form a complement to the nervous strain

caused by desk work. Any work to fulfil its proper function as ordained by nature, and not mutilated by man, must contain these complementary parts in itself.[47[pp.14–15]]

By making an inseparable bond between work and leisure, the development vision departs from modern forms of economic life that are based on a work-leisure dichotomy, which is visible in almost all sectors. The growing perception of 'work-life balance' is a clear example of such a dichotomy. Work and life are seen as two different spheres, where the former is considered as an act that provides monetary benefits, whereas the latter is recognised as a family responsibility.[49]

Access to energy is a crucial factor that decides the degree of self-sufficiency at the individual level as well as for the society at large. As Illich says, the kind of energy that is adopted determines the 'range and character of social relationships' in a society.[50[p.5]] Essentially, energy is central to political economy.[50[p.49]] Inaccessibility of energy for work curbs the ability of individuals to be self-sufficient, and thus to self-rule. Hence 'human energy,' which is expended by the human body and enables individuals to do manual work, becomes the primary energy source in the economy of self-sufficiency.[47[p.24]] This is because it is the only energy source that can be accessed by everyone.

Further, human energy becomes an essential way for the equitable distribution of material wealth as it enables more people to own the means of production. The reason being, capital in the form of money is unequally distributed in the society whereas capital in the form of labour is more or less equally distributed. Therefore, any means of production that depends more on labour could create a more equal society by distributing wealth in its production stage itself. This goes against the wealth production and distribution mechanism of prevailing development models where wealth is created by a small group of people who possess monetary capital and the state is expected to distribute it among the masses. For example, the power loom that runs on electricity demands a few lakhs of rupees as investment and so becomes unaffordable to a large section of the society. Here, there are greater chances of enforcing the owner and labourer relationship and increasing the disparity between the rich and the poor. Whereas, handloom that works on human energy does not require more than a few thousand rupees of investment. This allows individuals from a large section of society to own it. Thus, human energy also becomes a way of attaining a sustainable future, as it is the most environmental-friendly, renewable energy source. Most importantly, human energy sets an inherent limit to production and consumption in the economy which is essential for the survival of our civilization on our finite planet.

It is essential to recognise that the energy that goes into the production process also defines the means of production. From this standpoint, the means of production can either be categorised as tool-based production, driven by human energy, animal power and the burning of wood, or machine-based production, which works on electricity and fossil fuels. The former falls into the classification of a 'current economy' whereas the latter into a 'reservoir economy.' Though self-sufficiency in the development vision embraces tool-based production as its primary means of production., machine-based production also has a specific place in this economy, particularly where there is a need for articles that require 'standardization' and 'precision' in large numbers.[4[p.168]]

Ownership over the means of production is crucial for self-sufficiency to function. The land, which is the primary source of raw materials for production, should be held in 'trust' by the state (participatory community) and 'leased out for a term of years, the extent vary[ing] according to the capacity of the tenant to handle the property to the best advantage as a trust' on behalf of the state.[43[pp.49–50]] The means of production are expected to be owned by the people, particularly producers, to ensure distribution of purchasing power across the society. However, state ownership is recommended over means of production that involves 'public utilities' as well as supplies of 'raw materials' and 'manufacturing instruments' necessary for enterprises owned by people.[4[p.151]] As well-known economist EF Schumacher points out, 'in large-scale enterprise, private ownership is a fiction for the purpose of enabling functionless owners to live parasitically on labour of others.'[51[p.267]] State ownership is considered appropriate because it is the only possible way for the masses to mobilise the considerable capital amount required for such a means of production.

The exchange of articles among people is the next crucial component of self-sufficiency. Since one cannot produce all material necessities, exchange becomes a means to fulfil one's material needs. Since human beings are bound in cosmic unity, any exchange must be mutually beneficial. Such an exchange is possible only when 'the buyer and seller are on equal footing.'[4[p.130]] Exchange based on money does not create such conditions, mainly when it involves the transaction of perishable, consumable goods. The imperishable nature of currency gives more bargaining power to the consumer because one can 'wait for any length of time' whereas the value of perishable goods that 'depreciate with time' forces the seller to 'come to terms quickly.'[4[p.125]] This naturally places the producer of perishable goods in a position of disadvantage while a consumer with imperishable money is in an advantageous position. Thus, exchange based on currency leads to inequality in society and perpetuates violence. On the other hand, self-sufficiency embraces 'barter' as a primary means of exchange that operates 'only on surplus' to 'reduce the chain of exchange and to bring the producer and consumer together,' placing them on a more level ground.[4[p.130,131]]

By considering labour as the centre of exchange, the development vision departs from modern economics which holds capital as the medium of exchange. However, it recognises the role of capital in the 'temporary storage of purchasing power' which brings convenience to exchange.[4[p.121]] Since money has become impossible to exclude from the modern world, the vision encourages individuals to follow the principle of barter by transacting their surpluses within their locality while using currency as the medium of exchange whenever barter is not feasible.[4[p.131]] The consumption of locally-produced goods through capital transaction 'virtually' makes it a barter exchange, where both parties can comprehend the impact of their transaction on each of their lives more accurately.[4[p.131]] Therefore, it ensures the right and obligation chain in the Natural Order. The development vision also advocates a living income for the producers, particularly during an exchange based on capital because, otherwise, one would end up in destitution and unable to self-rule.

Consumption, the next component of the economy, has a major role to play in self-sufficiency. Since every material transaction is a moral transaction, the development vision demands consumers be responsible for the indirect causes of their purchase. When someone buys an article, that person becomes a part of the impact that particular consumable has caused on society and the environment during its production. As Kumarappa writes:

> If a tin of cocoa is produced from nuts cultivated in West Africa, roasted and tinned in England, brought to India and sold here; if the cultivation takes place in Africa under the terms and norms of the slavery or indentured labour, and the roasting and tinning take place in England under sweated labour, and favourable customs and tariffs are afforded for the sale of this tin of cocoa by the government of India, because of the political power they hold here, then we buy a simple, harmless-looking tin of cocoa, we become parties directly for supporting the slave labour conditions in Africa, the exploited labour conditions of England and the political subjection of India. In the same manner as if one were to buy an ornament that has been taken from a child which had been murdered for it, one would become guilty or a party to that murder.[52[p.10]]

Therefore, it is the individual's responsibility to become '*Swadeshi*' or a consumer who consumes articles that are produced within one's sphere of cognisance.[4[pp.79–80]] In doing so, individuals fulfil both right and obligation in the Natural Order. As the distance between production and consumption increases, it becomes impossible for consumers to comprehend all the social and environmental impacts of production. Hence, it becomes necessary to 'limit our transaction to a circle well within our control,' where the 'smaller the circumference, the more accurately we can gauge the result of our action and more consciously shall we be able to fulfil the obligation as trustees.'[4[p.79]] For such local consumption, self-control is necessary for individuals—this could be gained by realising their embeddedness in the cosmic unity where 'every act of ours affects our fellow beings one way or the other.'[52[p.11]] Such self-control restrains overconsumption and encourages self-sufficiency.

Further, local consumption enables consumers to directly interact with producers to make articles according to their needs. These direct interactions between producer and consumer facilitate cooperation not just in economic terms but also in other aspects of their lives. It becomes a platform to understand the living conditions of each other and recognise their mutual obligations. It also leads to an active consumer by giving space to exercise one's creative faculties and promoting the originality of self-expression in both producers as well as consumers. By considering consumption as a way of self-expression and not just an ethical transaction, the development vision goes beyond the modern concepts of ethical trade and ethical consumption.

Disposal, which is the last component of the economy, is an important aspect of self-sufficiency. Every sentient being in nature is bound by the 'cycle of life,' which maintains its continuity through 'cooperation' with various other sentient and insentient beings, akin to the Earth's biogeochemical cycle.[5[p.2]] Any break in this cycle results in violence, 'ending finally in destruction.'[5[p.2]] Therefore, 'self-preservation' demands cooperation with the cycle of life.[5[p.2]] Individuals are expected to consciously ensure the disposal of goods without short-circuiting this cycle. In doing so, the right and obligation in Natural Order are fulfilled. Even though there is a significant overlap between economic self-sufficiency of the development vision and the contemporary concept of eco-localism, particularly in their emphasis on reducing the distance between production and disposal, they diverge in their precepts. The former prescribes a reduction in the distance between production and disposal from a moral standpoint whereas the latter advocates the same from a more material standpoint.

Notes

a The concept of the Great Chain of Being contains fundamental 'unit ideas' of plenitude, continuity and gradation bound by the teleological notion of perfection. The idea could be traced from Plato to Kant. 'Plenitude' is defined by Plato as the universe which contains every possible form of existence corresponding to different levels of perfection represented on the Great Chain of Being. Aristotle formulated 'continuity' which asserted that the universe is made of infinite series of forms where at least one attribute is shared between the next being in the form of 'gradation' from simple to complex. Being a strict teleological concept of the natural world, the degree of perfection achieved was defined by divine Providence. God was the epitome in the chain following angels. In this concept, God was the creator of all beings. The particular position for a being was assigned by God himself, and there was no space for evolution. The immutability was the dominating feature of western political economy discourses until Charles Darwin published his work on evolution in the middle of the 19th century.[6]

b The efficacy of such a non-violent democracy can be seen in the framing and implementation of a 'swaraj constitution' in the princely state of Aundh from 1938 to 1948.[29] The entire experiment involved a population of just over 76,000 scattered over 72 villages.[30[p.x]] According to some of the villagers who were part of the experiment, the overall governance of the state during the period was of 'the utmost satisfaction' to 'everyone.'[29[pp.6–7]] When India got freedom from the British, the princely state was merged into the Indian nation-state. This, according to Apa Pant, was 'a new torrent of history which swept away the germinating seedling that the Mahatma had prompted, the Raja had planted and which had been devotedly tended to by his dedicated people.'[30[p.xii]] Yet, the experiment stands as the most significant effort to implement a non-violent democracy.

c Taylorism is the management of workflow, particularly with an objective of improving labour productivity. It was advocated by Frederick Winslow Taylor in the late 19th century in manufacturing industries in the United States. Although the term is not popularly in use, the idea is widely adopted across different sectors in the world.

References

1 Gurney P. *Wanting and having: Popular politics and liberal consumerism in England, 1830–70.* Manchester: Manchester University Press; 2014.

2 Jessop B, Sum N-L. Pre-disciplinary and post-disciplinary perspectives. *New Political Economy* [Internet]. 2001 Mar 1;6(1):89–101. Available from: https://doi.org/10.1080/13563460020027777

3 Bryson G. The emergence of the social sciences from moral philosophy. *International Journal of Ethics.* 1932;42(3):304–23.

4 Kumarappa JC. *Why the village movement?* Wardha, India: All India Village Industries Association; 1936.

5 Kumarappa JC. *Economy of permanence.* Wardha, India: All India Village Industries Association; 1949.

6   Kutschera U. From the scala naturae to the symbiogenetic and dynamic tree of life. *Biology Direct.* 2011;6(33). https://doi.org/10.1186/1745-6150-6-33.

7   Gandhi MK. To American friends. *Harijan.* 1942 Aug 9.

8   Roy R. Modern economics and the good life: A critique. *Alternatives: Global, Local, Political.* 1992;17(3):371–403.

9   Warneken F, Tomasello M. Helping and cooperation at 14 months of age. *Infancy.* 2007;11(3):271–94.

10 Tomasello M, Melis AP, Tennie C, Wyman E, Herrmann E. Two key steps in the evolution of human cooperation. *Current Anthropology.* 2012;53(6):673–92.

11 Grove M, Coward F. From individual neurons to social brains. *Cambridge Archaeological Journal.* 2008;18(3):387–400.

12 Common Cause Foundation. Perceptions matter. 2016.

13 Warneken F, Tomasello M. Altruistic helping in human infants and young chimpanzees. *Science. American Association for the Advancement of Science*; 2006;311(5765):1301–3.

14 Boehm C. *Moral origins: The evolution of virtue, altruism, and shame.* New York: Basic Books; 2012.

15 Terchek R. *Gandhi: Struggling for autonomy.* Lanham, MD: Rowman & Littlefield; 1998.

16 Gandhi MK. *Indian home rule.* Phoenix, Natal: International Printing Press; 1910.

17 Gandhi MK. An appeal to the nation. *Young India.* 1924 July 17.

18 Gandhi MK. The greatest good of all. *Young India.* 1926 Dec 9.

19. Kumarappa JC. Liberal democracy in India. 1955.

20 Gandhi MK. Non-violent crafts. *Harijan.* 1940 Sep 1.

21 Kumarappa JC. *Science and progress.* Wardha: All India Village Industries Association; 1948.

22 Gandhi MK. On khaddar. *Young India.* 1926 Mar 18.

23 Bilgrami A. *Secularism, identity, and enchantment.* Cambridge, MA: Harvard University Press; 2014.

24 Kumarappa JC. *Planning by the people for the people.* Ahmedabad: Navajivan Press; 1954.

25 Yamunacharya M. *Studies in philosophy, religion & literature.* Bangalore: Prof. M. Yamunacharya Memorial Trust; 2018.

26 Kumarappa JC. *The unitary basis for a non-violent democracy.* Wardha: All India Village Industries Association; 1951.

27 Sale K. *Human scale revisited: A new look at the classic case for a decentralist future.* Vermont: Chelsea Green Publishing; 2017.

28 Gandhi MK. Independence. *Harijan.* 1946 July 28.

29 Rothermund I. *The Aundh experiment: A Gandhian grass-roots democracy.* Bombay: Somaiya Publications; 1983.

30 Pant N. *Introduction. An unusual raja: Mahatma Gandhi and the Aundh experiment.* Hyderabad: Sangam Books; 1989.

31 Bhargava R. Political responses to religious diversity in ancient and modern India. *Studies in Indian Politics.* 2013;1(1):21–41.

32 Kumarappa JC. Democracy—Formal or Dharmic? *Gram Udyog Patrika.* 1950 March.

33 Gandhi MK. Power not an end. *Young India.* 1931 July 2.

34 Gandhi MK. Gandhiji's walking tour diary. *Harijan.* 1947 Mar 16.

35 Kumarappa JC. *Swaraj for the masses.* Wardha: Akhil Bharat Serva Seva Sangh; 1948.
36 Gandhi MK. Cobblers v. Lawyers. *Young India.* 1921 Sep 29.
37 Gandhi MK. *Constructive programme: Its meaning and place.* Ahmadabad: Navajivan Publishing House; 1945.
38 Gandhi MK. Some rules of Satyagraha. *Young India.* 1930 Feb 27.
39 Gandhi MK. The Birmingham visit. *Young India.* 1931 Nov 5.
40 Gammon E. *Affective neuroscience, emotional regulation, and international relations. International theory.* Cambridge: Cambridge University Press; 2020.
41 Gandhi MK. Is this humanity? *Young India.* 1926 Nov 4.
42 Gandhi MK. When killing may be Ahimsa. *Young India.* 1928 Oct 4.
43 Kumarappa JC. *Vicarious living.* Madras: Kumarappa Publications; 1959.
44 Seymour J. *The complete book of self-sufficiency.* London: Transworld Publishers Ltd; 1978.
45 Princen T. *The logic of sufficiency.* Cambridge: MIT Press; 2005.
46 Alexander JK. *The mantra of efficiency: From waterwheel to social control.* Baltimore, MD: John Hopkins University Press; 2008.
47 Kumarappa JC. *The philosophy of work and other essays.* Wardha, India: All India Village Industries Association; 1947.
48 Seabrook J. *The song of the shirt: The high price of cheap garments, from Blackburn to Bangladesh.* London: C Hurst & Co; 2015.
49 Lewis S, Beauregard TA. The meanings of work-life balance: A cultural perspective. In: Johnson R, Shen W, Shockley KM, editors. *The Cambridge handbook of the global work-family interface.* Cambridge: Cambridge University Press; 2018.
50 Illich I. *Energy and equity.* London: Calder & Boyars; 1974.
51 Schumacher EF, Ernst F. *Small is beautiful: Economics if people mattered.* London: Harper & Row; 1973.
52 Kumarappa JC. *The Gandhian economy and other essays.* Wardha: All India Village Industries Association; 1949.

Part II

Swaraj Development in Practice

3 A Brief History of Khadi Sector

To demonstrate swaraj development in practice, I would like to take Khadi, the handspun and handwoven textile sector in Karnataka as an example, because of its historical connection with the Swaraj Development Vision. It is essential to provide a brief account of this relationship to fully appreciate my reasons for choosing the Khadi sector.

Archaeological evidence shows that cotton textile production in India dates back to 3200 BC.[1[p.2]] India was the largest cotton textile producer and supplier in the world until the advent of mechanised textile industries in Britain in the latter part of the 18th century.[2[p.14]] The Indian cotton textile manufacturing 'industry was a jigsaw of hundreds of thousands of small cotton farms, millions of households spinning yarn and weaving cloth, and exchanging their wares through small, periodic, local markets that also fed into larger world systems.'[2[p.2]] The substantial quantity of Indian textiles 'were not luxuries but was used as everyday attire and as decorative items by consumers of all social levels and economic standing.'[3[p.19]]

Indian cotton textiles were in high demand in foreign countries until the 19th century and had 'posed a threat to local textile manufacturers, who feared being displaced by competition', particularly in countries like France, Spain, Prussia and England.[4[p.405],5[p.273]] As historian Prasanna Parthasarathi states, Indian cotton textile 'clothed the world.'[6[p.32]] Their success in the global market came from their capacity to 'customize products to suit the tastes and preferences of differentiated markets.'[1[p.6]] According to historian Giorgio Riello, the production and consumption of Indian textile was a 'centrifugal system based on the diffusion of resources, technologies, knowledge and sharing of profits.'[3[p.7]] Such a global trade was operated based on cooperation and symbiosis, and was loosely connected by nodes of exchange.

DOI: 10.4324/9781003353096-6

The age of Indian domination in global production and trade of cotton textiles turned upside down with the emergence of Europe, particularly Britain, as the powerhouse of mechanised production in the latter part of the 18th century. In Britain, cotton became the basis for the broader Industrial Revolution. It was also the first commodity to enter a global production complex, with raw materials and labour drawn from around the world. The newly born 'empire of cotton' thrived on '[s]lavery, the expropriation of indigenous peoples, imperial expansion, armed trade, and the assertion of sovereignty over the people and land.'[7[p.xv]] Riello described it as "a centripetal system, one based on the capacity of the centre to 'exploit' resources and profit towards its productive and commercial core."[3[p.7]] The result was "[t]he 'great divergence'—the beginning of the vast divides that still structure today's world, the divide between those countries that industrialised and those that did not, between colonisers and colonised, between the global North and the global South."[7[p.xiv]]

The repercussion of the Industrial Revolution on the Indian cotton textile sector was disastrous. The once leading global exporter of cotton textiles became an importer of cheap cotton yarn and, finally, the cloth itself. The British empire exercised its political power, often violently, to suppress the Indian cotton textile sector, forcing people to buy cotton clothes produced in Britain. The result was a decline in the earnings of those employed in the sector and a deterioration in their standard of living.[4[p.399]] According to RM Martin, a British administrator in Bengal in 1832, 'by increase of export of cotton goods to India from Britain many millions of Indo-British subjects have been totally ruined.'[4[p.400]] Around the same time, the then governor-general William Bentick declared 'the misery hardly finds a parallel in the history of commerce. The bones of cotton-weavers are bleaching the plains of India.'[4[p.401]]

The concept of development in terms of material accumulation was the driving force behind this empire of cotton that was built on morality of self-interest, political centralisation and economic efficiency. The new system was based on competition, exclusiveness, global exploitation of natural resources, slavery and markets coordinated by rising European financial centres. Furthermore, the focus was more on the material that was produced rather than the lives of people involved in the global cotton supply chain.

The emergence of the Khadi movement in India in the early 20th century was a reaction to the empire of cotton in Britain. However, it was not just a movement to bring back the lost glory of Indian cotton textiles. It also had a broader vision of overthrowing the empire of cotton as well as constructing an alternative development path for the country that would prevent other such empires from arising in the future. The movement was ignited by Gandhi, with his conception of development as swaraj as the driving force behind it. The Khadi sector, conceived as a material quest as well as a spiritual/moral quest to establish a non-violent social order, was considered as a platform to demonstrate the Swaraj Development Paradigm.

As a part of the exercise, Khadi was not simply revived, but refurbished to suit the normative vision of the Swaraj Development Paradigm. The definition of development in the Khadi movement sought a shift to the moral plane once basic material needs were fulfilled. Built upon morality of the greatest good of all, political decentralisation and economic self-sufficiency, the Khadi movement stood in stark contrast to the organising principles of the empire of cotton. It became a visual symbol of the Indian freedom struggle. It also became the first social movement in modern India to bring poverty to the centre stage of national consciousness, and make livelihood an issue of mass mobilisation.

By the early 20th century, when Gandhi returned to India from South Africa, the Indian textile sector was ruined by the Industrial Revolution. The task of rejuvenating the sector required a serious effort of re-establishing long-severed supply chains, carrying out brand-building exercises and technological interventions. Further, addressing the criticisms of Khadi was crucial to establishing a positive social consciousness about the movement and, in turn, bringing more people into the fold.

Initially, the Khadi movement began with the intention of providing a supplementary livelihood for a rural workforce that had been deprived by the colonial rule. It was initiated by Gandhi through the *Satyagraha Ashram*, which was founded in 1915 in Ahmedabad, a popular place for handweaving. The principal objective of the *ashram* was to help residents learn the handweaving process and to explore ways of making it an aspirational profession. By 1917, the *ashram* had seven looms providing livelihoods for 17 people.[8[p.44]] The following two years proved that weaving, a caste-based occupation, required special skills. In contrast, the activity of hand spinning on the *charkha* (spinning wheel) was seen as relatively simple, offering a vocation that could be performed irrespective of gender, caste or religious affiliations. Therefore, the focus of the *ashram* shifted more towards hand spinning, and by 1919, it became the most visible feature of the community.[8[p.47]]

A breakthrough in the spread of Khadi came from the Rowlatt *satyagraha* launched by Gandhi in early 1919. The movement was against the Rowlatt act passed by the imperial authority, which effectively authorised the government to imprison without trial any suspects involved in revolutionary activities. The central element of the movement was the adoption of the *swadeshi* pledge that required shunning cloth manufactured from anything foreign, be it machinery, raw cotton or yarn. This, in turn, increased the sales of Khadi[8[p.49]] and the *ashram* started to coordinate with many spinning and weaving clusters to supply the growing demand. The *satyagraha* acted as a launching pad for Khadi and brought it out of the confines of the *ashram* and into a wider public realm.

The next breakthrough for Khadi came from the non-cooperation movement pioneered by Gandhi against the British empire in 1920. It was a reaction to a chain of events caused by the empire. First among them was the Jallianwala Bagh massacre, which took place in 1919. The British Indian army, under the command of brigadier general Reginald Dyer, fired rifles into a crowd of peaceful civilians who were condemning the arrest of national leaders under the Rowlatt Act. The massacre took a toll of at least 370 lives. Second was the administrative brutality in Punjab in 1919 as a response to the Khilafat Movement. This movement was led by Indian Muslims to pressure the British government to preserve the authority of the Ottoman Sultan as Caliph of Islam following the breakdown of the Ottoman Empire after World War I.

As a part of the non-cooperation movement, similar to the Rowlatt *satyagaraha*, an appeal was made to the public to boycott foreign articles and adopt the use of locally made goods. It successfully mobilised people from different sections of the society and Khadi became a symbol of Indian independence. The collective spinning brought women out of their confined domestic roles into the political realm. According to scholar Sujata Patel, it was a movement that liberated Indian women.[9] It also brought youth into the fold of the Khadi movement by asking them to withdraw from government-owned and affiliated educational institutions.

Later, in 1920, the Indian National Congress led by Gandhi instituted the All India Tilak Memorial Swaraj Fund, setting the target of raising Rs 10 million to bring more people into the fold of the freedom struggle. It embarked on a task of enrolling 10 million primary members in the political front and took up the task of distributing 20,00,000 *charkhas*.[8[pp.84–5]] Additionally, schools and colleges that were run by nationalist leaders introduced spinning as a part of their curriculum. [8[p.79]] A six-month course on weaving was also designed and offered at the Satyagraha Ashram in 1923.[10[p.101]]

The colonial government's reaction to the non-cooperation movement was to imprison Gandhi and other nationalist leaders. A few months after his release in 1924, Gandhi demanded that the Congress Party make wearing Khadi mandatory for all its members. He also demanded the passing of the spinning resolution, which required a minimum of 2,000 yards of self-spun yarn per month from each of them, if they were to retain their primary party membership.[8[p.140]] The resolution was passed despite opposition raised by many. The party instituted the All India Khadi Board (AIKB) to carry out the mammoth task of collection, transmission and keeping track of subscription yarn. However, the spinning franchise did not last long due to the lack of conviction and commitment among members.

The failure of the Congress Party to carry out the spinning resolution prompted Gandhi to establish the All India Spinners Association (AISA) in late 1925 to undertake the work of promoting Khadi. Hundreds of independent Khadi production and sales centres emerged in different parts of the country due to the constant effort of AISA. Further, AISA established its own production and sales units to become the largest Khadi institution in the country. By 1926, AISA was providing work to 110 carders, 42,959 spinners and 3,407 weavers through 150 production centres catering to the needs of some 1,500 villages. It peaked in 1941, directly affecting the lives of 2,75,146 villagers, including 19,654 Harijans[a] and 57,378 Muslims scattered across at least 13,451 villages. It managed to distribute 'more than four and a half crores of rupees' (approximately $5,68,217 in current exchange value) among its employees up to 1944.[11[p.10]] Although AISA ran like any other commercial firm, it succeeded to some extent in fusing commerce and sentiments of philanthropy. The average wage for its workers was Rs 0.83 per day while the country's average wage was Rs 0.67 per day in 1927.[8[p.206],12[p.240]] Towards the end of 1946, it had increased to Rs 1.5 per day when the country's average wage was Rs 1.21 per day.[8[p.206],12[p.241]]

However, AISA had to face many serious obstacles. To begin with, it was a challenge to work with a mass of illiterate, unskilled, secluded and destitute producers.[8[p.233]] It was also a struggle to find workers because of the insufficient remuneration caused by the uphill task of marketing Khadi products for higher prices. Therefore, retaining workers, in the long run, was not easy. The growing reluctance of weavers to use handspun yarn, due to its low strength compared to mill spun yarn, mounted a further significant challenge. It became difficult to convince the younger generation to take up Khadi activity since they increasingly perceived it as a backwards-looking technology.[8[p.234]]

An intensive branding exercise was essential to create a demand to sustain the rising Khadi production. The exercise was rigorously carried out by Gandhi, who made use of traditional metaphors imbued with moral overtones and facts from the past that were amply supported by historical research. For example, he stated:

> In my eyes, Khadi is artistic enough. Khadi has the property of absorbing moisture. Khadi's roughness was particularly suited for being used as a towel, as cleansing the body with it after a bath stimulates the skin. Khadi is more useful and superior cloth. It is more beautiful than calico because it has a soul in it. There is some craftmanship at any rate in the making of Khadi. Just as no two leaves of a tree are exactly alike, no two lengths of handspun, hand-woven Khadi can be so.[13]

Further, he set the narrative of wearing Khadi as a 'national duty [that] occasioned sacrifice of art and aesthetics, tastes and fashion, choices and colours' to evoke patriotic vigour among the consumers.[8[p.52]] He encouraged them to buy Khadi for home furnishing if it was not convenient for someone to wear. He also sought out prominent men and women to be brand ambassadors of Khadi. It resulted in a demand for Khadi from as far as Baluchistan, the Nilgiris, and even Aden. The narrative set the tone for the adoption of the *charkha* as a symbol in the Congress flag while Khadi caps became a site of conflict between loyalty to the empire and patriotism to the country. Public bonfires of foreign cloths were organised in different parts of the country to bring social consciousness into the fold of the Khadi movement. The imperial government confronted the looming movement by turning Khadi-wearing into a penal crime and imprisoning Khadi wearers, particularly during the early days of the non-cooperation movement. It also took further disruptive measures such as the sealing of Khadi outlets, forceful shutdown of production centres, detention of Khadi workers, freezing of bank accounts among others.

As part of the brand building, Khadi exhibitions were organised during the annual sessions of the Congress party. It was a space to exhibit improved Khadi technologies and showcase various Khadi products. It became a distinctive feature of the sessions. From 1934 onwards, the Congress exhibitions were jointly organised by AISA along with the All India Village Industries Association (AIVIA), newly formed by Gandhi and led by Kumarappa to expand the constructive work programme. The first ever full-fledged exhibition of Khadi and rural industries became a reality at the Lucknow Congress session in 1936.[8[p.178]] Besides aiding Khadi sales, the exhibitions also became a means for the Congress Party to reach out to the masses.

However, with the increase in demand for Khadi, AISA started facing a shortage of supply. As a result, spurious Khadi invaded the market.[8[p.131]] The Indian textile mills took advantage of this and sold their manufacture as Khadi to credulous customers. Many hand weaving clusters started using mill-spun yarn for the warp and handspun yarn for the weft. The penetration of such mix Khadi into the market posed a significant threat to the movement.

So, as a counterstrategy, Gandhi issued leaflets informing people of the real intent and texture of Khadi. He insisted that volunteers very politely put this leaflet into the hands of all persons who were not clad in Khadi. Descriptions of Khadi should be written on large wooden boards, and big leaders and non-hired men should parade the streets wearing these, he said. In fact, 'Gandhi himself offered to roam one hour every day in the Ahmedabad market with a board suspended on his neck.'[8[p.84]] He also advised Khadi shops to appoint experts who could differentiate between handmade and machine-made fabrics to check authenticity.

Further, AISA secured the authority from the Congress party to issue certification authenticating the quality of Khadi. With this, a fabric with the AISA stamp was considered as the only authentic Khadi, and the rest as spurious. The AISA also appealed to consumers to buy certified Khadi only from authorised *Khadi bhandars* (sales outlets). Additionally, AISA claimed a patent for 'Khadi' and 'khaddar.'[14] All these efforts helped shaped a brand for Khadi. By 1929, there were about 328 *Khadi bhandars* across the country.[8[p.223]] However, in later years, AISA faced a severe challenge from consumers increasingly complaining about the lack of quality, durability and convenience. From 1944 onwards, Gandhi started to emphasise more on 'economic self-sufficiency' by recommending the reduction in the distance between production and consumption of Khadi as far as possible.[11[p.6]] Further, he started to advocate decentralisation of power within AISA by terminating its Khadi certification process as well as withdrawing from direct production and marketing of Khadi. Instead he wanted to encourage people to set up their own Khadi enterprises taking 'the entire responsibility' while 'recogni[sing]' the 'authority' of AISA 'only in the moral realm.'[11[p.33]]

Technological intervention was an essential aspect of the Khadi movement. There was an awareness that high capital-intensive technologies would eventually lead to the concentration of wealth in the hands of a few. Therefore, the key concern was to come up with technologies that were more efficient but simple, comprehensible, run on a local resource base and affordable to the masses. Initially, in 1919, Gandhi announced an award of Rs 5,000 to those who could invent an efficient *charkha* that would enable spinners to earn more. Although the task was taken up by many individuals and organisations, nothing much came of it. However, it encouraged many people to continue the task of improving the spinning wheels, resulting in a display of 15 types of spinning wheels in the spinning wheel exhibition in 1921.[8[p.122]]

The efforts to encourage technological innovation continued to be expanded. In 1930, Gandhi instituted a price of Rs 100,000 to encourage the invention of an improved *charkha*, and the competition was thrown open to foreign nationals as well. The conditions included 'easy portability, capable of being worked by hand or by foot in an ordinary Indian village home, availability at a price not exceeding Rs 150, and working life of about twenty years. The replacement charges of worn-out parts per year were not to exceed five percent of the cost of the machine.'[8[pp.121–2]]

However, the inventions created as part of the competition could not meet the criteria. Eventually, Gandhi insisted on devoting more energy towards making the ancient pattern of *charkha* more durable, cheaper and portable, rather than waiting for a 'revolutionary *charkha*.'[15] As part of the drive for technological innovation, *Saranjam Sammelans* (technical conferences) and *Prayog Charcha Sabhas* (forums for discussion of experimental initiatives) were organised.[10[p.10]] Gandhi also inaugurated a *Khadi Vidyalaya* (Khadi research and training centre) in 1941 to undertake scientific studies and improve Khadi technologies.[8[p.214]]

The movement gave rise to numerous technical literatures. For example, *Khadi Samachar Patrika* was the first journal published by *Sabarmati ashram*.[8[p.129]] There was *a Khadi News centre* that issued leaflets with relevant information about production and sales.[8[p.130]] Further, Maganlal Gandhi wrote a weekly column in Gandhi's *Young India* under the title of 'Khadi notes' to report the results of the experiments carried out at the *ashram*.[10[p.102]] Gandhi himself wrote a set of articles in his *Harijan* magazine explaining Khadi science.[16–18] Later, AISA brought out a periodical called '*Khadir Katha*' to publish interrogative reports that explored the causes for the decline of Khadi.[8[p.217]]

Several technical books were also published as part of the drive for technological intervention. The first book titled '*Charkha Sastra*', a detailed description of Khadi techniques, was published by Maganlal Gandhi in 1924.[10[p.52]] Richard Gregg, an American lawyer, along with Maganlal Gandhi, wrote a book named '*Takli Teacher*' in 1926 with illustrations and texts to popularise the idea of spinning. Gregg also published a book called '*Economics of Khaddar*' which made the argument for Khadi.[19] A book called '*Charkha Sangh ka Navasamskaran*' was published in Hindi by AISA in 1948 just before the death of Gandhi, highlighting the ideology of Khadi activity.[8[p.261]]

The Khadi movement was not free of criticism. Opposition was heard from the outer circle of the Khadi movement, close comrades and even from within the inner circle. Addressing their criticisms was a constant process. Outsiders, particularly individuals from the educated classes, were sceptical about Khadi and its role in the Indian freedom movement. For example, Aurobindo Ghosh, who got into spirituality after an initial involvement in military activities against the British Empire, asked Gandhi whether he would face an army in the ongoing World War II with his *charkha*. Mohammad Ali Jinnah, who became the founder of Pakistan, had a similar opinion too.[8[p.180]]

Moreover, Gandhi's insistence on handmade processes created a sense of anti-industrialisation among the educated Indian class. The *Leader,* an Ahmedabad-based journal, stated that the Khadi movement was an effort towards 'putting back the hands of the clock of progress by attempting to replace mill-made cloth and mill-spun yarn by hand-woven and handspun yarn.'[20] Educated Indians saw 'constructive programme, including Khadi, as a painful distraction from the main task of political liberation.'[8[p.184]]

Opposition also came from close comrades such as Jawaharlal Nehru, who became the first prime minister of Independent India. He asserted that Khadi workers were apolitical and not a key part of the broader national freedom movement.[8[p.180]] He even accused Khadi of being anti-industry and anti-modern. Tagore, a polymath from Bengal, criticised the act of bonfires and accused Gandhi of playing with people's emotions.[10[p.88]] He also stated that undue prominence was being given to *charkha* in the freedom movement, causing harm to the nation by stunting its intellectual growth. A similar argument was placed by MN Roy, a socialist comrade who declared that spinning was nothing but a waste of energy.[10[p.89]]

Equally hard questions were raised by individuals from within the Khadi movement when the outcomes were not meeting their expectations. This mainly included those who had worked with Gandhi and accompanied him in Khadi activities. For example, George Joseph, a Khadi worker, argued that Khadi activity was unjust to consumers as well as producers because it was too expensive to buy. He contended that Khadi workers, particularly spinners, were underpaid to an extent that it was not even sufficient for their physical maintenance.[21[pp.412–3]] Similarly, S Ramanathan, secretary of the Tamil Nadu branch of AISA, 'disapproved Khadi and advocated khaki, representing militarisation, as a political weapon.'[8[p.186]] He also claimed that the spinning wheel was surviving on artificial respiration provided by Gandhi, and that Khadi harks back to primitive times by rejecting mechanisation. EV Ramaswamy Naicker, who was the president of the All India Khadi Board formed by the Congress party, and the father of the self-respect movement in Tamil Nadu, declared that Khadi was a 'superstition of the recent origin' and was more dangerous because it was charged with patriotism.[8[p.187]]

Gandhi patiently refuted the criticisms thrown at the Khadi movement. He repeatedly responded by stating that swaraj was not just about a power shift from British hands to Indian hands. Instead, he emphasised, it was about establishing a social order devoid of all forms of exploitation, which he described through the mythical phrase of *Ramarajya*. He made the argument a potent force to silence his critics, particularly those who questioned his leadership in the Indian freedom movement for placing Khadi at its centre. To the objections raised on bonfires, Gandhi responded that it was a plea for recognising the dignity of human labour. He stated that he did not make a distinction between ethics and economics, thereby pointing to the role of the intricate relationship between morality and materiality in shaping the living condition, as discussed in the previous chapter. He further proclaimed that 'in burning my cloth, I am burning my shame'. According to Sabyasachi Bhattacharya, the bonfire was an action of 'retirement within ourselves, a refusal to cooperate with English administration on their terms.'[22[pp.99–121]]

To the critics who termed spinning as a waste of energy, Gandhi replied by providing favourable reasons for spinning, such as, it was the readiest occupation known to thousands of people, easy to learn, did not require much capital, implementation was easy, was cheaply made and provided immediate relief.[23] Gandhi responded to the criticisms of Khadi being anti-industrialisation and anti-modernity by emphasising the need for machines that do not displace human labour.[24[p.377]] He argued that *charkha* is the most appropriate technology for liberating people and addressed the concerns raised against the economic viability of Khadi by calling such criticism as a sign of impatience.

With the arrival of freedom, and the subsequent assassination of Gandhi, the institutions founded by him, such as the AISA and AVIA, were merged under a larger umbrella organisation called the *Sarva Seva Sangh*. Further, the All India Khadi and Village Industries Board (AIKVIB) was set up by the newly formed Indian government to promote and support Khadi and village industries across the country. The AIKVIB was renamed as the Khadi and Village Industries Commission (KVIC) in 1957, and was conferred a legal position under the Ministry of Small and Medium Enterprises (MSME). As a result, the Khadi movement evolved into a bureaucratic department within the vast hierarchy of the newly formed government. The sector was organised according to a formal economic planning based on estimates and targets. The focus shifted from the original intention of creating a non-violent social order to a race towards increasing productivity. Currently, the KVIC and the state-level Khadi and Village Industry Boards (KVIBs) regulate Khadi production and marketing through independent Khadi institutions comprising artisans from across the country. Today however, despite decades-long efforts by the government, the Khadi sector is staring at a severe crisis and on the verge of collapse.[25–31]

Notes

a Harijans are the member of an outcaste group in India formerly known as untouchables.

References

1 Riello G, Parthasarathi P, editors. *The spinning the world: A global history of cotton textiles,* 1200–1850. Oxford: Oxford University Press; 2009.

2 Menon M, Uzramma. *A frayed history: The journey of cotton India.* New Delhi: Oxford University Press; 2017.

3 Riello G. *Cotton: The fabric that made the modern world.* Cambridge: Cambridge University Press; 2013.

4 Parthasarathi P, Wendt I. Decline in three keys: Indian cotton manufacturing from the late eighteenth century. In: Riello G, Parthasarathi P, editors. *The spinning world: A global history of cotton textiles, 1200–1850* (pp. 17–42). Oxford: Oxford University Press; 2009.

5 Riello G. The globalization of cotton textiles: Indian cotton, Europe, and the Atlantic World, 1600–1850. In: Riello G, Parthasarathi P, editors. *The spinning world: A global history of cotton textiles, 1200–1850* (pp. 261–87). Oxford: Oxford University Press; 2009.

6 Parthasarathi P. *Why Europe grew rich and Asia did not: Global economic divergence,* 1600–1850. Cambridge: Cambridge University Press; 2011.

7 Beckert S. *Empire of cotton: A new history of global capitalism.* London: Penguin Books; 2015.

8 Ramagundam R. *Gandhi's Khadi: A history of contention and conciliation.* New Delhi: Orient Longman; 2008. 298 p.

9 Patel S. Construction and reconstruction women in Gandhi. *Economic and Political Weekly.* 1988;23(8):377–87.

10 Prasad CS. *Exploring Gandhian science: A case study of the Khadi Movement* [Unpublished]. [New Delhi]: Indian Institute of Technology; 2001.

11 Gandhi MK. *Reorientation of Khadi.* Thanjavur: Sarvodaya Prachuralaya; 1964.

12 Leeuwen B van. *Human capital and economic growth in India, Indonesia, and Japan: A quantitative analysis, 1890–2000.* Eindhoven, Netherlands: Bas van Leeuwen; 2007.

13 Gandhi MK. Uses of Khadi. *Young India.* 1920 Apr 25.
14 Gandhi MK. Khadi in the legislatures. *Young India.* 1929 Mar 28.
15 Gandhi MK. Notes: New spinning wheel. *Young India.* 1922 Jan 19.
16 Gandhi MK. How to begin? *Harijan.* 1937 Apr 10.
17 Gandhi MK. What is khadi science? *Harijan.* 1937 Jan 16.
18 Gandhi MK. What khadi workers should know? *Harijan.* 1937 Feb 13.
19 Gregg RB. *Economics of khaddar.* Madras: Ganesan S; 1928.
20 Gandhi MK. Swadeshi. *Young India.* 1920 Aug 18.
21 Gandhi MK. A military programme. *Young India.* 1929 Dec 19.
22 Bhattacharya S. *The Mahatma and the poet.* New Delhi: National Book Trust; 1997.
23 Gandhi MK. Waste of energy? *Young India.* 1924 Aug 21.
24 Gandhi MK. The Poet and the Charkha. *Young India.* 1925 Nov 5.
25 Busenna P, Reddy AA. Khadi and village industries: A case study of khadi institutions in India. *Journal of Rural Development.* 2011;30(3):273–89.
26 Comptroller and Auditor General of India. Report of the comptroller and auditor general of India for the year ended March 2013. Government of India; 2014. Report No.: 25.
27 Mohammad N. Between ghost artisans and mechanisation, how many jobs does the khadi industry really generate?. *The Wire* [Internet]. 2018 [cited 2019 Oct 16]; Available from: https://thewire.in/economy/between-ghost-artisans-and-mechanisation-how-many-jobs-does-the-khadi-industry-really-generate
28 Planning Commission. *Evaluation study on khadi and village industries programme.* New Delhi: Government of India; 2001.
29 Dhanuraj D, Nair L, Varghese JP. *How to revive the Khadi sector—An evaluation with special focus on Khadi act.* Kochi: Centre for Public Policy Research; 2018.
30 Nair LR, Dhanuraj D. *Evaluation of government interventions in khadi sector.* Kochi: Centre for Public Policy Research; 2016.
31 Goel N, Jain K. Revival of Khadi—An analysis of the state of khadi in India with supply and demand side problems. *Innovative Journal of Business and Management.* 2015;4(5):100–3.

4 An Interpretive Analysis of Khadi Sector in Karnataka

In this chapter, I would like to discuss the existing living conditions in the Khadi sector by using the Swaraj Development Vision, outlined in Chapter 2, as a lens. This chapter delves into the interpretive fold of the swaraj development approach discussed in Chapter 1. Even though different dimensions of the Khadi sector such as morality, politics and economy have been explored in separate sections, it is essential to keep in mind that they are not exclusive from one another.

Fieldwork spanning an entire year was carried out in Karnataka between September 2017 and August 2018 as a part of the exercise. Numerous visits were made to different Khadi institutions, including the Khadi and Village Industries Commission (KVIC) and the Karnataka State Khadi and Village Industries Board (KSKVIB) to gather preliminary information based on the Swaraj Development approach. Multiple methods such as purposive sampling, snowballing, observations and semi-structured interviews were used to gather relevant data from the field. The arguments and discussions made in Chapters Four and Five are based on what was heard, observed and experienced in the production centres, marketing outlets, the KVIC and the KSKVIB offices. The names of people and places in these chapters have been kept anonymous to protect the informant's privacy as well as to ensure the wellbeing of the respondents and communities.

Morality

The living conditions within the Khadi sector are significantly shaped by the morality of its community. The morality or the sense of right and wrong among people involved in the Khadi sector is deeply rooted in their cosmological visions. This cosmology is considerably shaped by the normative values 'impose[d]' by their cultural memory[a] rooted in their religion and religious practices.[2[p.6]] The following word cloud

DOI: 10.4324/9781003353096-7

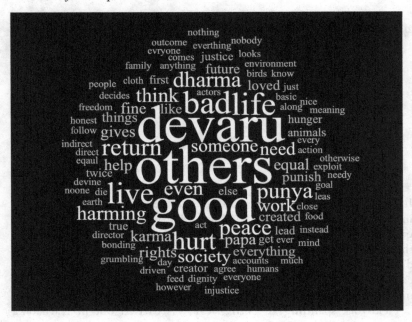

Figure 4.1 Word cloud representing the morality of Khadi sector.

(Figure 4.1) represents the top 100 words that were emphasised by Khadi workers while discussing morality.

Although there is a slight difference among the worldviews of Khadi workers from different social positions, a majority of them believe that the world we live in is driven by the power of God or *devaru* in Kannada, as is prominent in the word cloud above. There is a deep-seated belief in the conception of God, and the statement that '*devaru* is there' is often repeated while discussing their worldviews. God is perceived as the pantheon of many Gods and local deities. Mariyappa, who has been working as a warper for the last 13 years, humbly says, 'God has created humans and all other beings. So, everything has equal right to live.' The Khadi workers' cosmology gives the ultimate agency to God while recognising limited agency of human beings. Shanthamma, a weaver at a small Khadi production unit in a remote village, concludes her tirade against God with the words: 'God is there to take care of justice.' The burden of providing justice, after human efforts to do so ends, is left to God. Further, there is an understanding that, as human beings, we have to perform actions without expectations, and it is unto God to determine the final outcomes. As Chaluva, a differently abled bobbin winder, states, 'Our job is to constantly work, and he [God] decides its rewards.' There is an underlying notion of divine providence that is widely present among the members of the khadi sector and is seen to connect individuals despite other differences in beliefs.

The cosmology of Khadi workers entails hierarchy. God is perceived as supreme at the top of the cosmological chain. The hierarchy within the human society is enforced through the conception of caste, especially among people from the dominant Hindu religion. The conceptions of God, patriarchy and caste are directly derived from their cultural memory. Further, no clear relationship is ascertained between humans and non-human beings in their cosmology. 'Non-human beings have equal rights. However, they lead their own lives, and we lead our own lives' says Sarojamma, a spinner in her forties. Similar opinions are held by a large section of the Khadi community.

There is, however, a recognition of the 'other' in the conception of the individual in the cosmology of Khadi workers. This is particularly visible in their notion of 'good.' There is a general sense that one's good is connected with the good of others. Rachappa, a worker in the Central Sliver Plant (CSP), whose clothes are covered in cotton dust and who must raise his voice to make his point audible over the harsh sounds of the blow room machine, avers, 'Good means not hurting others.' This particular understanding of good is widely present among people irrespective of their social positions. It shows the embeddedness of the 'other' in their cosmology.

As shown in the word cloud, Khadi workers give the most emphasis to 'others' while describing their notion of good. This indicates that although the bodily identity of the self is central to their conception of individual, the notion of obligation to others is implicitly present and is perceived as more important than the notion of right or self. Sharadamma, a widow working at a Khadi production unit, stops her weaving to express with conviction: 'Hurting others is sin. If someone comes to us hungry, first we should satisfy him by giving what we have saved for ourselves.' Similarly, Mahadevamma, an older illiterate woman, who winds the bobbins, says, 'When we do something, it should not hurt others, instead it should help them.' Such a belief is not only restricted to people from the dominant Hindu religion but is also expressed by Khadi workers who follow Islam. Suhana, a newly married woman, utters even as her focus remains on her stitching work, 'Good means loving and helping others even if we do not have enough for ourselves.' Thus, the cosmology of Khadi workers advocates a conception of the individual that prioritises obligation over right while acknowledging the presence of both self-interest and altruistic nature in human beings.

The tapestry of tales of Gods in local lore is a key source of moral codes. Khadi workers, like Jayamma, an elderly bobbin winder, find their lives resonated in such stories. She says, 'Even the Gods have been through all kinds of situations, so what about us mere mortals?' The conception of karma (action) offers a basic framework for their morality. According to them, what a person chooses to do is of concern only to them. For example, if a person misuses what was given to them, then it is reflected in their *karma*, and God keeps an account of such wrongdoings. However, the responsibility for these misdeeds can be accepted by the wrongdoer, and atoned for. There is a strong understanding of *dharma* (right action) that encompasses the act of not hurting others and of helping the needy. In other words, as Kumarappa suggests, *dharma* is an action that does not produce 'conflict.' In their cosmology, following *dharma* results in *punya* (merit or peace) whereas disobeying *dharma* results in *paapa* (demerit or discontent).[3[p.26]] However, the indirect consequences of their actions on others are not paid much attention in their everyday life.

The non-violent relationship between the self and the other in the Khadi community's cosmology springs more from fear than love, as envisaged in the Natural Order of the Swaraj Development Paradigm. Basappa, a senior weaving supervisor, seated on a broken wooden chair, says, 'We should not even think about harming others because it will return to us in the future.' Such a fear is often associated with the conception of God. Deepa, a young tailor from Dalit community, utters without a second thought, 'If we hurt others, God will punish us in some way or the other. We do not get to know how.' There is a strong underlying belief that whatever action we pursue in the world, it will eventually affect our own lives. Therefore, the morality of non-violence in the cosmology of Khadi workers is rooted in a fear of harm that can befall the self.

Furthermore, such a morality based on non-violence is limited in scope due to the cosmological hierarchy provided by conceptions of patriarchy and caste. Shanthavva, a spinner in her fifties working on a broken cement floor, says 'Once my daughter gets married, she will work as her husband says.' Such an acceptance of male superiority among Khadi workers is widespread. However, women, particularly young adults, appear more aware of male domination in the society. In between bites of her lunch, Bhavya, a 27-year-old weaver, says, 'Even though my husband and I speak to each other before taking any decision, I feel that a man's point of view dominates the society.' Such an attitude is common not only in rural settings, but in urban spaces as well. 'Domination of men is equally prevalent in cities. Even though I have done my diploma, my husband does not allow me to work outside. I work here only because he also works here,' 34-year-old saleswoman Manjula avers in Kannada with a smattering of English words. Even though a small section of women in the Khadi sector are aware of the society's male-centric ideology, they are afraid to resist because they perceive such an act as a challenge to their accepted cultural norms.

Similarly, the limited scope of the morality of non-violence is visible in the case of caste. According to Ratnamma, a middle-aged spinner:

> We talk to *Dalits*.[b] But since they eat non-veg, we do not go to their homes. If their wedding is in marriage halls, then we go. Otherwise, we do not. They also do not touch us and do not enter our houses. They do not even touch our utensils. We can walk in their streets wearing slippers, but they cannot [do so] in our streets because they are from a lower caste. God has created caste and we have to follow. If an educated *Dalit* enters our house, we look after him, but once he leaves, we do what we have to do. We clean the house and do not use the utensils that were used by him. If we see from his standpoint, what we do is wrong. However, it is our tradition. We cannot do anything about it. If we touch them, others in our community do not touch us.

The above-mentioned perspective on caste is quite common within the Khadi community. There is a strong sense that they are obligated to follow their cultural norms. They believe that questioning practices that are part of their long-standing cultural tradition is inappropriate. They also fear of being ostracised from their social groups if they do not follow such practices. However, a contrary opinion on caste is held by a small section of the Khadi community. Nirmala, a young block printer who has managed to study up to high-school explains:

> There are only two castes. One is male and the other is female. Everything else is created by us for our self-interest. There was discrimination based on caste before but not now. The caste [experience] is more in villages, not in cities. We go to the house of Muslims and they come over to our places. Here all are working-class people and you cannot discriminate. In villages, there are separate places for people of different castes but that is not the case here. Even if one has a discriminatory attitude, one cannot show it in a city because you will not know who the other person is. For us,

speaking [to one another] and friendship is more important, not the caste. Do we take our caste with us when we die? If a Dalit becomes a minister, do we not allow him into the temple? Now, he is even allowed to go directly near the God's idol.

Although modern education has contributed to changing views on caste, during the same conversation Nirmala added, 'Our daughter will be married to a person from our caste.' Such a contradiction shows the deep-rooted ideas of caste within the cosmology of Khadi workers.

While caste has resulted in exclusion, domination and inequality (as discussed), it has also provided stability, social identity and a support network to individuals. As Madamma, a middle-aged weaver from the *Dalit* community states, 'If anything happens, our community [caste] is there for our support.' Similarly, Rama, a spinning supervisor from the *Kuruba*[c] community says, 'I participate and assist in all the events of our [caste] people. Similarly, they reciprocate when my family holds a function or when there is a need.' The community or caste bonds are reinforced through gatherings at marriages, deaths and other functions. Caste has become a social net for individuals to overcome hard times and has also given freedom to different communities to practice their customs and beliefs. Shwetha, a weaver from the *Vokkaliga*[d] community, states, 'We [Vokkaligas] have our own Gods and festivals.' Similarly, Sannakka, a spinner from *Dalit* community, says, 'Although there are many common festivals, we [different castes] all have our own Gods, rituals and festivals.'

The conceptions of patriarchy and caste show the 'inherent tendency' of cultural memory to provide a hierarchical and elitist structure to the society rather than an egalitarian one.[1[pp.116–7]] The main reason for such a tendency can be discerned in the 'intra-cultural diglossia,' in which practices, opinions and conventions that people harbour are moulded by the interaction between elite and folk traditions over generations.[1[p.116]] However, as demonstrated above, cultural memory 'does not just mutilate people and knock them into shape' but also 'develops forms of life, opens up possibilities in which the individuals can invest and fulfil [themselves].'[2[p.6]]

Development and Prosperity

A vast section of the Khadi community perceives development in terms of material accumulation. Mahadev, the secretary of a Khadi institution, who sits on his desk in front of an old picture of Gandhi inside a broken frame says: 'Development is enhancing one's comforts in life. For example, having a nice house to live in, a car to travel, a good cell phone and so on.' Similarly, according to Mohan, an officer at the Khadi and Village Industries Commission (KVIC), who wears a machine-made outfit, 'Our country is getting developed. Now we have highways, metros, hospitals, airports like any other Western country.' Such a materially centred understanding of development among Khadi workers has been shaped by the globalisation and urbanisation policies of the Indian state, coupled with the agendas of international actors such as the World Bank, the World Trade Organisation and the International Monetary Fund.[5[p.143],6[p.181]]

Furthermore, media advertisements and the entertainment industry have created material discontent and escalated the desire for greater material possessions.[7–10] It reflects, what Kumarappa states, 'advertisements and high pressure salesmanship' that create artificial wants among individuals and lead them to dissatisfaction in life.'[11[p.63]] Even though people involved in the Khadi sector have a materially centred understanding of development, it is largely considered as a means to attain peace in life, which is a non-material end. Put differently, they perceive development in terms of material accumulation as the primary means to accomplish prosperity defined in terms of peace. There is a widespread belief among the Khadi community that the purpose of life is to experience peace. This is illustrated in the case of Boramma, a senior weaver working for the last three decades at a Khadi institution. She states, 'If we harm others, then we will not have peace. Then what is the point of life?' Likewise, Gururaj, a young salesman at a dilapidated Khadi outlet says, 'How can we hurt others? Do we not need peace in our lives?'

Politics

The analysis of power in relation to the social positions of the workers can help us understand the intricacies within the larger social fabric in which the Khadi sector is embedded. The power distribution within the Khadi sector is profoundly shaped by the social positions determined by intersectional factors such as gender, age, education, financial status and social group. A majority of the Khadi workforce is made up of women, a representation which follows the larger gender composition within the Khadi sector—62.64% women in Karnataka and 80.39% across the country.[12[p.44]] Men, meanwhile, have mostly occupied key managerial positions in Khadi institutions. As pointed out by scholar P Gopinath, this shows the 'in-built gender inequalities and the biases in these hierarchies' and the prevailing patriarchal view within the Khadi community.[13[p.328]] In contrast to the over-representation of women in primary production occupations such as spinning, weaving and stitching, the workforce at the Central Sliver Plant (CSP) is dominated by men.

The gender roles imposed by culture is one of the critical factors for such a skewed representation in the Khadi sector. Cultural practices of khadi workers have obligated women to deal primarily with household management while compelling men to act as breadwinners. Therefore, there is considerable pressure on both genders to fulfil their roles in the existing social order. However, as breadwinners, men are enabled more social mobility compared to their female counterparts. This makes it easier for men to take up occupations that demand flexibility in work time and workplace. For example, the key positions of power in Khadi institutions demand frequent business travel to different places. Given the customary gender roles, it is easier for men to undertake such work since they are not required to remain at one place. In contrast, most of the women, particularly in rural areas, find it unmanageable since they are rooted in everyday household work and cannot free themselves from chores like cooking, fetching water, washing clothes, sending children to school and so on. Similarly, the CSP which operates throughout the day requires people to work in all three shifts every month. However, the situatedness of women in the social order does not easily allow them to work particularly during the night shifts, as it could disrupt their household responsibilities.

Further, the existing gendered social order is exploitative of women. There is growing violence against women in the country. A report on crimes against women in India by the National Crime Records Bureau shows that a total of 89,097 cases were registered in the year 2018 alone, with 31.9% of cases related to 'cruelty by husband or his relatives' followed by 27.6% connected to 'assault on women with intent to outrage her modesty.'[14[p.xii]] The cases of 'kidnapping and abduction of women' stood at 22.5% while rape cases comprised 10.3% of the overall crime figures. Sexual harassment of women by male strangers in public spaces is a widespread and serious problem in the country.[15] Therefore, there is a sense among women that going out at night could increase the risk of getting attacked by men in addition to a prevalent culture of victim-blaming. The result is an overrepresentation of men in key positions of power and in the CSP.

The intersection between culturally prescribed gender roles and the degree of income generation from various occupations is another essential factor that shapes gender representation in the Khadi sector. The primary occupations within the sector like spinning, weaving and stitching are seen as sources of additional income and have largely failed to provide 'subsistence wages.' This is precisely why men find it impossible to undertake such activities because then they cannot fulfil their responsibility as breadwinners.[13[p.334]] Whereas owing to a fixed workplace and flexible work timings, these occupations are more often taken up by women as they can be performed in conjunction with the double burden of household duties that are culturally expected of them in rural Karnataka. The result is a disproportionate representation of women compared to men within the Khadi community.

Age is another crucial factor that has moulded the Khadi sector. People across age groups—from early adulthood (20–30 years old) to old age (65 years old and above)—are involved in Khadi activity. A majority of people fall under the category of mature adulthood (middle age), which ranges between 30 to 65 years old, and from which all of the key power positions in the sector are populated. The second most prominent age group are the elderly, who are chiefly occupied in non-power positions such as bobbin winders. The early adulthood age group generally occupies non-power positions such as spinning and weaving, and are a minority in Khadi community. This particular age group representation is down to several reasons.

The responsibilities of sustaining a family and raising children have compelled people, especially from the mature adulthood category, to undertake Khadi occupations unlike the other age groups. There are not many work opportunities available in rural Karnataka to fulfil their expected familial responsibilities. For example, agriculture, a predominant occupation in the state, is in severe crisis. It has become economically unviable because of misguided government policies, increase in production costs due to labour crisis, water scarcity, the over use of fertilisers and pesticides, soil infertility and frequent failures to get remunerative prices for produce in the market that often depends on inequitable international trade agreements.[16,17] Similarly, cattle rearing, the other prominent activity in rural Karnataka that has traditionally provided the much-needed cash flow, is also facing challenges. It has increasingly become a capital-intensive occupation due to the hybrid cattle breeds that require a shed to maintain ambient temperature, frequent medication and specially formulated industrial feed,[18–20] making it cost prohibitive for the financially weaker sections. Apart from agriculture and livestock rearing, people in rural Karnataka do not have other livelihood options, since most of the rural industries have been eroded due to the growth of mechanised production units in urban areas. Therefore, Khadi has become the only option for many people in rural Karnataka.

In addition to the scarcity of livelihood opportunities, Khadi workers, who have hardly had some years of schooling, prefer working indoors rather than toiling in the hot sun. For example, Bhagya, a 37-year-old spinner who has completed her high school education, says, 'I think I am not strong enough to work outside. I prefer to work under the shade. So, I simply work here.' Such notion of a lack of stamina to work in the fields is persistent among large sections of women involved in Khadi activity. Further, given the physical labour required in agriculture and livestock rearing, they are perceived as lowly occupations within the society.

Khadi activity, though, has supported the elderly who are struggling to keep up with the increased pace and complexity of life that has emerged with the advent of commercial agricultural practices.[21] According to Ravi, who owns a boutique store and is a close associate of one of the Khadi institutions:

> The elderly people in rural Karnataka are shunned both by society and the family. Most of these older women usually sit in a corner. The youngsters in the family are always hooked to mobile phones, and others to the television. They neither have a voice to say which serial they want to watch nor anybody to talk to them. If you see the architecture of those spaces, they will be sitting on the veranda, and even food will be brought on a plate to the same place. Unfortunately, their situation is same as that of dogs that roam outside of our houses.

Lakshmamma, an 80-year-old bobbin winder, expresses a similar feeling. She says, 'I work here because I can talk to people. Otherwise, I have to sit alone in my home.' This shows that there is a lack of social engagement for old people within their homes as well as within the villages. As a consequence, Khadi activity, mainly spinning and bobbin winding, has become the most dignified job they can find in the village. Therefore, Khadi has become a means of engagement, a place for social interaction and also a small source of income for elderly people to meet their domestic expenses.

Formal education, or lack thereof, is another crucial factor that has shaped the Khadi community. According to the 2011 census, the literacy rate in Karnataka is 75.6%, with nearly 82.85% males and 68.13% females.[22[p.8]] Individuals who have graduated from universities make up a small minority in the Khadi sector. But a majority of the Khadi workers are illiterate or have had a few years of schooling and it is them who carry out most of the primary occupations that involve physical work. In contrast, a majority of the key positions of power in the sector that are seen to entail intellectual labour are occupied by individuals who have studied up to secondary school level or above.

The low literacy rate in the Khadi workforce reflects the level of formal educational attainment in Karnataka, which has an average gross enrolment ratio of 82.2% across primary, upper primary and secondary school levels, and 28.8% in higher education.[23[p.47],24[p.6]] There is a clear inverse relationship between modern education and the willingness to perform physical work. Therefore, the representation of people with little to no schooling is predominant in the sector, which involves a significant amount of physical work. As Savitha, a middle-aged spinner, says, 'Our children should pursue education and become officers. Otherwise, they have to work like us.' Similarly, Girish, a 26-year-old weaver, states, 'I am looking for an office job in the government because there will be no risk and life will be settled.' This corroborates Kumarappa's claim that the prevailing education system has produced people with a 'clerical mind' that carries out the 'orders of others' instead of self-governing people who possess 'initiative and original thinking.'[25[pp.174–5]] Such an understanding of education, as a way for obtaining better employment opportunities that are devoid of physical work, is widely persistent among Khadi community.

The perception of seeing physical work as an undignified job has created a much larger social crisis. It has made it difficult for individuals who perform physical work as part of their livelihood to find life partners. Vinay, a warper at a Khadi institution, explains,

> Everyone in my family is insisting that I move to Bengaluru, at least until I get married. It is difficult these days to find a bride who wants to stay back in the village. They prefer grooms who are settled in the city and are even happy to marry someone doing menial job like a watchman's. But they do not want to get married to a farmer or a weaver settled in a village. To top it all, for someone like me, who has a dark complexion, it is even more difficult to find a bride.

This social crisis of finding life partners is one of the major forces pushing the younger generation to leave rural spaces.

A large section of the Khadi community falls into the category of Below Poverty Line (BPL).[e] They are the people who are not in a position to have independent livelihoods. However, for most of them, a

Khadi occupation is a source of additional income. As Kaveri, a spinner who hails from the BPL category, says

> I am a widow and I live alone. Since I have got a BPL card, I get free rice from the government ration store and here I earn some money for *sambar* [stew] to eat it with. That is how I am surviving.

Khadi has become a lifeline for many such destitute individuals. Those occupying positions in the Central Sliver Plant (CSP), the Karnataka State Khadi and Village Industries Board (KSKVIB), the Khadi and Village Industries Commission (KVIC) and the managerial positions at Khadi institutions largely come from the Above Poverty Line (APL) category.

Religion is another important factor that has shaped the situatedness of individuals within the Khadi sector. A predominant section of people within the assessed Khadi community are from the Hindu religion while a few are from the Islamic and Christian faiths. Such representation is the result of the dominance of the Hindu religion in the broader social fabric as well as the greater freedom for women of this faith to work outside of their homes compared to the latter, particularly Islam. Khadi workers also come from different caste categories.[f] However, a majority of them are from 'Other Backward Classes' (OBC), which chiefly includes several different intermediary castes in the caste hierarchy. The second-largest section of people is from the 'Scheduled Caste' (SC) and 'Scheduled Tribe' (ST), which mainly comprises castes that are at the bottom of the caste hierarchy. A small number of Khadi workers come from the 'General' (GEN) category, which primarily consists of castes that are at the top of the caste hierarchy.

As a major chunk of the workforce in the sector is from the Hindu religion, the cultural memory formed by the nexus between caste and hereditary occupation has significantly shaped their degree of participation. Such a memory encompasses a sense of belonging to their caste, familiarity with certain occupational skills and experience with their caste-based vocation. The cultural memory of people from caste groups that were traditionally involved in the textile manufacturing sector has enabled as well as discouraged them from undertaking Khadi activity.

While their familiarity with the fine-skilled physical labour involved in textile manufacturing has led many of them to readily consider Khadi occupations, for many others, their painful past experience with the collapse of the traditional cloth manufacturing sector with the advent of mechanised textile sector has discouraged them from taking up Khadi activity as a livelihood. Rangaswamy, a weaver who was associated with one of the Khadi institutions, says, 'I will not let my son Ravi take up our traditional weaving occupation. I have ruined my entire life sitting on this handloom.' Experiences like these indicate that 'remembering our past can also give rise to current emotional experience.'[27[p.201]] In other words, the present social behaviours of individuals are significantly shaped by their past experiences. On the other hand, cultural memories without such past experiences, specifically in case of people from other caste groups, have meant a more open-minded approach towards exploring the Khadi sector. According to Shruthi, a young weaver at a Khadi institution, 'I am from the community of carpenters. I had never done weaving before. So, I thought of giving it a try. Although it was difficult the first few months, now I find it easy to do.' For people like Shruthi, it is moving beyond the sense of belonging that they have towards their caste-based occupations and to acquire unfamiliar physical skills, which in this case is for the Khadi activity.

This power distribution demonstrates the role of the dialectical relationship between morality and materiality in shaping the social positions of Khadi workers. For example, elements of their morality can be observed in the obligations that bind them, such as their commitment to uphold gender roles, familial responsibilities as individuals grow older and the duties that arise from being part of a particular social group, especially a religious one. Similarly, material conditions such as water scarcity and soil infertility have significantly lowered livelihood opportunities available in rural Karnataka to become an important factor that decides the level of people's participation in Khadi sector.

The power dynamics—the way power operates in terms of decision making within the Khadi sector—helps to understand its degree of decentralisation and the level of control that Khadi workers have over their lives. This also provides insights into the level of non-violent democracy that exists within the sector as aspired to by the Swaraj Development Paradigm. The production and marketing of Khadi without obtaining recognition from the KVIC is deemed illegal in the country. By securing the word 'khadi' as a registered trademark, KVIC is claiming an exclusive right over its use. The process of authenticating Khadi involves affixing the Khadi mark tag and labels issued by the KVIC on all Khadi products that are produced and sold. No textile can be traded under the name of Khadi in any form without this Khadi mark.[28[p.12]] By making this a requirement, the state has centralised the power and, in turn, exerted a considerable amount of control over the participation of individuals in the sector.

The state has taken control of Khadi production to retain its authenticity due to its historical value. Individuals who are interested in setting up a Khadi production unit have to make an application to the

KVIC with extensive documentation. Vinod, a boutique store owner who wants to set up his own Khadi production unit, says,

> The registration rules are so stringent that it is not possible for individuals like me to start the activity in a small way. For example, it is mandatory to have 25 spinners, five weavers and two supervisors to start the activity. Where can I find so many skilled people at once?

It is evident that such a requirement to start Khadi activity is impractical.

Technology upgradation in Khadi production is another important area of state intervention. Setting up Central Sliver Plants (CSPs), introducing improved spinning wheels and peddle looms, initiating solar spinning wheels and solar looms to increase productivity are some of the significant efforts that are being made in this regard. Madan, the secretary of a Khadi institution, says, 'Introducing the new model spinning wheel is a great intervention. It has helped spinners to produce more good quality of yarn.' However, according to Charan, the secretary of another Khadi institution, 'Although the CSP has helped Khadi institutions to procure raw materials, Khadi institutions have lost the freedom to decide what kind of cotton has to be used and what kind of yarn has to be produced.'

Even though technological interventions have helped Khadi production to some extent, in many cases they have not yielded the desired results. Maheshwari, a weaver, points out,

> A few months back, all the traditional frame looms were replaced by improved peddle looms provided by the government. You just have to peddle and not use your hands in the weaving. But these new looms are not at all user-friendly. That is why we are asking the supervisor to reinstall the traditional looms.

Similarly, Gangamma, a spinner in a remote village, says, 'Recently we got a few solar spinning wheels and looms. Initially, they were working fine but they broke down after a few months. Since nobody knows how to fix them, we have dumped them all in that corner.' This is indicative of insufficient technical support and services for the new machinery. More importantly, as scholar Shambhu Prasad points out, the KVIC's attempts at efficiency-driven technological interventions for enhancing productivity have 'increased the dependence on expertise from outside the Khadi sector' and have led to 'a loss of autonomy in technical matters' among the Khadi community. [29[p.222]]

The state not only controls the production of Khadi but also its sale. It is necessary to obtain a certificate from the KVIC for sales and the certification process is especially stringent. Explains Guru, a boutique store owner,

> I would like to sell Khadi in my store. However, the process is so strict that it is difficult to work it out. You need to change your store name and use the 'Khadi India' brand of the KVIC. Further, you are not allowed to make any value additions to the products sourced from Khadi institutions, and it is not possible to change the price of the products sourced from them. With all these rules, how can we run a successful Khadi store?

Similar to the certification process for Khadi production, even the certification for Khadi sales is based on misguided regulations.

The state also gives financial assistance through the KVIC and the KSKVIB to Khadi institutions in the form of incentives, loans and grants. Hemanth, the secretary of a Khadi institution, remarks, 'It is impossible to run Khadi activity without the financial aid of the state. We have survived solely because of government support.' The financial assistance provided by the state is largely based on a prior set of production targets, which the Khadi institutions are forced to abide by. In reality, aside of providing financial assistance, the state also demands that Khadi institutions follow strict guidelines on how funding is spent. This has created an enormous pressure on Khadi institutions to meet their production targets and has curbed their freedom to take independent decisions. By doing so, the state has breached the self-rule of the institutions and people involved.

The power relation between independent Khadi institutions and the state is a double-edged sword. For Khadi, a labour-intensive activity, the price of its products is substantially more expensive compared to those produced by the handloom sector, which uses machine spun yarn, and the power loom sector, which involves automation. Therefore, selling Khadi in the competitive market is a significant challenge for institutions. Hence, they look for financial assistance from the state to subsidise their production costs and to maintain lower market prices. Although this arrangement has helped Khadi institutions to market their products better, they have ended up losing their financial freedom. Therefore, a large portion of decision-making power in the sector lies with the state rather than with Khadi institutions. As Sunil Ray points out, it has "lent credibility to the 'parasitic relationship' of the Khadi institutions with the government", where the former look to the latter

for 'everything from production to sales.'[30[p.791]] As shown in the flow
chart (Figure 4.2) below, the Khadi sector is exceptionally hierarchical.
In addition, it is a sector 'over-regulated' by the state because of its perceived historical significance.[31[p.3]]

The Khadi sector has a top-down decision-making mechanism, with
a significant amount of power concentrated at the top. As such, the sector deviates from the Swaraj Development Paradigm, which emphasises
consensus-based decision making. The KVIC and the KSKVIB operate
like any other state apparatus, with executive and legislature divisions.
The former positions are filled through regular recruitment process of
the state whereas the latter are filled by the political party that forms the
government. The lack of space within the state machineries for individuals who possess first-hand experience in Khadi production and marketing has created a disconnect between the decision making and the

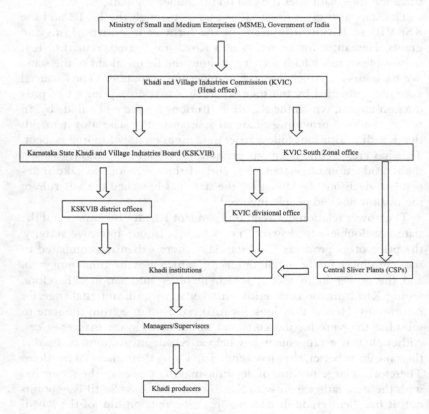

Figure 4.2 Political structure of Khadi sector in Karnataka.

complexities on the ground.[32] As a result, management decisions do not represent the 'grassroots realities.'[33[p.4]] The recruitment process, too, is clouded by bribery and favouritism based on caste and religion rather than passion for the work. For example, Anand, an officer at the KVIC, says:

I have a degree in commerce. I studied at a residential school run by a Hindu religious group. After I passed the entrance exam, I had to go through an interview for the post. I told the head of the religious group about the first-round selection. He directly called Delhi, and I got selected in the interview. They asked me simple questions like who the chief minister is, the finance minister is, the president is, where the Indian flag is produced and so on. If not for this intervention, they would have asked me more difficult questions.

Independent Khadi institutions do not have any stake in the decision-making process within the government wing. This centralisation of power has resulted in several problems. It has bred rampant red-tape across the system. For instance, the enormous paperwork involved with centralisation has increased the burden on Khadi institutions. Sujith, a clerk at a Khadi institution, opines, 'We should get rid of the government's financial aid. They are asking for more and more data every year. They demand more paperwork than the support they give us.' This results in significant delays in the release of funds to institutions. As Manjunath, a first division clerk at one of the KSKVIB district offices, explains,

Khadi institutions are expected to provide all documents of funds utilisation at the end of every quarter. However, these institutions do not have people to carry out clerical work. Since the paperwork takes a lot of time and effort, instead of submitting every quarter, they submit records once a year. That is why the process gets delayed from our end.

Centralisation has increased exploitation in the form of corruption at various levels. A significant share of allocated funds are 'being eaten by the government machinery rather than reaching the artisans.'[31[p.13]] As an evaluation report of the Planning Commission points out, 'only 58% of what the government spends on a Khadi unit reaches the Khadi workers'; the rest is appropriated by higher authorities and utilised for the managerial charges of the Khadi institution.[33[p.7]] According to Madan, the secretary of a Khadi institution, "Nothing works particularly at the KSKVIB if you do not bribe the officials. Even if you submit all the paperwork necessary for getting a grant, they remove a few papers from what you have given them and ask you to resubmit proper records. This happened to us once and we had to sit day and night reworking an entire year's worth of bills. This is how they tire you out if you do not 'look after' them well." Guru, the owner of a boutique which has successfully gained the trust of Khadi patrons over the last 10 years, laments:

> I have been sourcing Khadi materials from KVIC-certified Khadi institutions for the last ten years. When the KVIC made the Khadi mark compulsory for the sale of Khadi three years back, I tried to get it. I made several visits to the local KVIC office. Not once did they adequately direct me in this regard. Mine is not an isolated case. It has happened to many of my friends who own boutiques. Some have been asked for bribes to be granted the Khadi mark. The whole process was very tiring. Every time I was asked to bring new documents. My friends were asked to send material samples to check their authenticity were rejected, even though they were sourced from KVIC-certified Khadi institutions. Now I have received a letter from the KVIC questioning the use of the word Khadi in my brand without their permission. It is very discouraging. I have been thinking of shifting from the Khadi sector to the handloom sector.

Many people who hold managerial positions in Khadi institutions believe that corruption is found not only in the bureaucracy of the KVIC and the KSKVIB but also within the Khadi institutions. Hemanth, a secretary at one of the Khadi institutions, explains:

> Earlier, Khadi institutions used to get financial aid based on their annual sales. So, many Khadi institutions would submit bogus sales bills also give commissions from the released grant to the bureaucrats for accepting these fake bills. Later, in 2010, with the intention of curbing corruption, the grants were connected to production targets instead of sales. Since then, Khadi institutions must get the production target fixed every year from the KVIC. Based on the target, they allot funds. If Khadi institutions do not meet the pre-fixed production target, then they lose a portion of money in the grant they are supposed to get. So now, many Khadi institutions show bogus production figures on paper and get the grants released. Either way, commission and bribes for bureaucrats have become a

rule to get things done. Since Khadi institutions and bureaucrats are both corrupt, it works fine.'

The over-regulation by the state has also 'resulted in creating inefficiencies in the sector.'[31[p.2]] Aravind, a clerk at a Khadi institution, says, 'The financial aid does not come on time. There are cases where it has taken a couple of years to receive the sanctioned grants.' This reflects 'a significant time lag between the formulation and implementation of various policies in the Khadi sector.'[34[p.102]] Further, the hierarchy within the sector has become a barrier for effective implementation of government schemes such as insurance for Khadi employees, scholarships for children of artisans and so on. Often, schemes have not reached the intended beneficiaries and there is a lack of awareness among Khadi workers about the various benefits offered to them by the state.

Even though many bureaucrats agree that there is corruption in their system, a large section of them deny the allegations that are made by the Khadi institutions. Giridhar, a clerk at the KVIC divisional office, asserts, 'We fall under the central government. So nobody can entertain corruption.' The argument of a corruption-free system due to their association with the Government of India is widely present among bureaucrats at the KVIC. People at the KSKVIB also claim that their system is corruption-free. Shashank, an officer at the KSKVIB says, 'There is no corruption in our board because we do not make any kind of direct cash transaction. Everything happens online.' This is a statement often heard among bureaucrats to justify the KSKVIB's working.

It is evident that corruption is a rampant phenomenon in the country and has even become a 'way of life.'[35[p.242]] India was ranked 80th out of 198 countries in the Corruption Perceptions Index produced by Transparency International in 2019.[36] As anthropologist Akhil Gupta points out, the state machinery in India has a 'unique culture of corruption that mixes forms of horizontal and vertical corruption rarely seen together in other national contexts, affecting poor and rich alike, but in very different ways.'[37[p.1883]] Horizontal corruption is the extraction of large sums from a small number of transactions by government elites from corporate and commercial firms, whereas vertical corruption is the extraction of small amounts from large number of transactions from citizens in everyday life. The Khadi sector is a classic example of this unique culture of corruption, because it significantly involves 'welfare spending' where both forms of corruption often meet.[37[p.1879]]

Alongside red-tapism, corruption and payment delays, the existing political system has also failed to meet the needs of producers who are at the bottom of the hierarchy. There is no precise and robust mechanism in place to share their opinions and suggestions with those at the top, despite the producers being the end beneficiaries. For example, Girijamma, the spinner, says, 'To whom do we tell our problems? Higher authorities, politicians, bureaucrats, journalists just visit and go. They do not hear our plight.' Sharada, a weaver, adds, 'Every year many people come from cities like Bengaluru and take pictures sitting on looms and posing with bobbin-winding machines. However, nobody does anything to help us.' Such comments indicate that the centralised power relation has made Khadi producers mere spectators. As S Rohini states, 'the most glaring oversight in the current activities of the KVIC is that the empowerment of the spinners, weavers and artisans has not been in the forefront.'[38[p.13]]

There is a similar power relation in the CSP, which is run directly by the KVIC. The manager, who is a part of the KVIC's bureaucratic system, holds the power of managing day-to-day activities of the unit, as a result of which decision making is highly centralised. Even though it is a small unit of a few dozen people, there is no participatory space for workers in the decision-making process. Despite being a public enterprise, there is a similar relationship between primary producers and the managers as in the case of private enterprises that rest upon an owner and labourer dichotomy. There is a telling hesitation to speak to outsiders while higher authorities are around. As Gupta, one of the workers, tells me, 'You come early morning before the office hours. Then you can talk to anyone. The managers will not be here.' The entire workforce at the CSP has been filled by the KVIC through the regular recruitment process of the government. However, the same issues of centralisation, such as red-tape, corruption and failure to fulfil the needs of primary workers, are evident here too. Nagaraj, a worker at the CSP, says:

As far as I know, the rule is to buy cotton from the Cotton Corporation of India (CCI). Instead, the manager procures cotton from private players with whom he has a connection. A tender will be called, and whoever gives the highest commission to the manager gets the contract to supply cotton to the CSP. These private players do not follow required cotton standards. I have seen cases where the same party participates in the tender process with three different names and gets the contract. There is similar corruption in identifying contractors from sourcing water for cotton processing to the disposal of waste cotton. There is a guideline that good quality cotton should not produce more than five percent of wastage. Since low-grade cotton is being bought from private players, the waste is higher. So, adjustment will be made in the accounts. These corruption stories are never-ending. If there is a hole in a shirt, we can cover it, but if the entire shirt is full of holes, what do we do then? We have already gone too far. Ninety percent [of the system] is already rotten. Nothing can be done.

To the question of cotton sourcing, Aravind, the manager of the unit, says, 'The cotton rate at the CCI is expensive and we do not have funds to afford it. That is why cotton is being bought from private players. Although the cotton quality is not good, it is manageable.' However, a large section of workers holds the opinion that there is corruption at the management level. Vivek, a worker at the CSP, states,

The corruption starts from the allocation of funds in the budget itself. For example, half a million rupees will be kept aside for machine repair. However, they spend only a portion of it and appropriate the rest by showing fake bills. Several times, I have observed Khadi institutions complaining about the low quality of rovings[g]. Since the unit manager is on good terms with the KSKVIB and the KVIC officials, the Khadi institutions are forced to shut up.

There is widespread discontent among CSP workers about their work conditions, and they express feelings of helplessness and a lack of power to bring positive change at the workplace. 'Khadi means *khao khao*,' says Sanjeev, a worker. The word 'khao' means 'eat' in Hindi. It is used by many workers to describe the corruption that they see as synonymous with Khadi. The centralised political system has failed to meet the necessities of the workers. For example, the impact of cotton dust on their health is a significant concern. Most of them believe that they have developed respiratory and other related problems due to the fine cotton dust that is emitted during the production process. It is a well-known fact that long-term exposure to cotton dust results in substantial adverse chronic respiratory effects.[39,40] However, they have not been able to resolve this issue with the management. According to Gopinath, a worker:

It is challenging to work in cotton dust. It has impacted all our lives. While working, you cannot breathe if you wear a mask to prevent the dust. So, the dust absorption system which is in place must run continuously. However, we are not allowed to use it. If we switch it on, the manager will scold us. He says that the cotton dust absorption system cannot be run continuously because there is a budget deficit to pay the electric bills, and that running it for a few hours a day is enough to remove the cotton dust.

When the issue was raised with the manager, he responded saying, 'Running the cotton absorption system for a few hours a day is enough to remove the cotton dust. The problem is they do not wear masks while working, even if we constantly insist them to do so.' What this shows is the lack of a suitable platform for workers to voice their concerns to the management.

The Khadi institutions, being the primary production and marketing units of the sector, have followed a similar pattern of centralisation of power as in the case of the CSP. These institutions are legal entities registered under cooperative and societies act. The hierarchy within the institutions consists of three tiers: lower-level primary producers, mid-level managers and the top-level working committee. The primary producers are spinners, weavers, dyers, block printers and tailors, depending on the institutions. The managers look after the day-to-day activities of their respective production centres and sales outlets. The working committee is an elected body that manages the entire institution. The size and composition of the working committee are expected to be as per the regulations of the act under which the institution is registered. Furthermore, it is also expected to incorporate the model bylaw prescribed by the KVIC, according to which the size of the working committee should be anywhere between 9 to 15 people, and require two-fifths of the total members to form a quorum.[41] All the institutions that were studied fulfilled these criteria.

The workers and other Khadi supporters identified by the working committee act as the primary members of Khadi institutions. They elect directors to the working committee as well as the secretary, the most powerful position within the institutional framework. The selection process is based on a majority voting system. In doing so, it departs from the Swaraj Development Paradigm that emphasises decision making based on consensus. In most cases, people who are sympathetic to some influential individuals are elected to the working committee and the position of the secretary. Caste, religion and gender play a significant role in the election of directors. Manjunath, a salesman at a Khadi institution, states, 'Power always gives preference to people from one's own caste. For example, the last three secretaries have been from the *Lingayat*[h] caste.' Similar factors are also at work at the level of production centres. Pavithra, a bobbin winder, claims, 'The supervisor has given bobbin winding tool to whom he favours, including newcomers from his caste. I have been working here for decades, but he has overlooked me.'

Corruption within the institution works at different levels. According to a retired secretary of one of the Khadi institutions:

People run bogus Khadi institutions. It is more in silk and wool Khadi compared to cotton Khadi because they are not obligated to buy raw material from Central Sliver Plants. They show production cost and details of the artisans only on paper. In reality, they purchase ready materials from the market and sell it as their own brand. Often, they do not even sell it but show the same stock and take subsidies from the government. For a few years, they will show one side of the towel until dust piles up, and then they turn it around and show the other side as if it is new stock.

The notion of bogus Khadi institutions is pervasive among people who are in managerial positions. They think that most Khadi institutions are producing and selling fake Khadi. Sharath, the secretary of a Khadi institution claims,

I have seen many Khadi institutions using mill yarn for the warp and Khadi yarn for the weft. There are cases where Khadi is produced using mill yarn on power looms. Corruption is everywhere. People in power make money out of everything. Not even one percent of people are honest in the Khadi sector.

Similarly, Chaluvaraj, the president of a Khadi institution, recounts,

Once, the CEO of KSKVIB had come to our institution. I told him that I could show him three Khadi stores on the same road that only open at night. 'Why?' he asked. I replied, 'To write bogus bills!' You cannot get rid of corruption in the Khadi sector. The bureaucrats at the KSKVIB and the KVIC themselves will guide you on how to make money from different government schemes.

This resonates with a claim made by scholar D Dhanuraj that there are many Khadi institutions that have 'emerged only for getting KVIC rebates and other benefits but have not produced any Khadi product.'[28[p.6]] Further, Dhanuraj notes, 'while there is a demand for Khadi, it is unwittingly being met by spurious products, and the sale of such products is taking place because of the government's restrictive practices.'[31[p.9]] Such opinions highlight the role of the centralisation of power in perpetuating malpractice.

There is a strong perception of corruption in the working committee among primary producers. Since workers are not appropriately informed about the different government schemes and because of delays in dispensing the credit of various incentives, they feel that they are only getting a portion of the financial support while the rest is being usurped by the working committee. Gowramma, a spinner, says, 'Sometimes we get more wages and sometimes less. Supervisors are grabbing our money.' This isn't entirely untrue—there are opportunities for managers to misappropriate workers' wages. A retired manager of a Khadi institution points out, 'Workers are mostly illiterate. The management get their signatures by telling them a nice fake story and pocket their wages.'

The decisions within the working committee are taken by majority voting. This again contravenes the Swaraj Development Paradigm that stresses consensual decision making. There is a lack of active participation by the working committee directors in carrying out the activities of the institution. Many of them visit the institution only occasionally and make little effort to improve the conditions of the workers. Hari, the secretary of a Khadi institution, says:

> Directors are not actively involved. Instead of giving suggestions and working to improve the state of the institution, they always ask me to come up with solutions. Currently, we do not have a working capital and are in a state of bankruptcy. In the last meeting, instead of helping to raise working capital, they were asking me to do it. How many roles can I juggle by myself? I am already working as a secretary, accountant and salesman.

Such a lack of engagement and attentiveness by directors is evident in all the Khadi institutions that were studied. Often, the representatives of spinners and weavers in the working committee know little about their role as directors. They believe that their role is to mostly present the grievances of workers in the meetings instead of figuring out ways to improve the overall condition of the institution. Jayamma, a spinner representative in a Khadi institution, explains,

> I am one of the board directors. I attend meetings and raise issues about wages and the quality of raw materials. However, whenever I bring up the question of increasing wages, instead of exploring options, they show audit reports to convince me that it is simply not possible.

The usage of words such as 'they' to imply the working committee is extensively observed among representatives and underlines the fact that their concerns are not taken seriously within the committee. The promotion of individuals to higher positions within the institution is primarily based on their work experience and managerial skills. However, there is a strong sense of abuse of power, especially by the secretary in most institutions. The misuse of power involves silencing adversaries, giving promotions to their loyalists, nepotism and corruption. In large institutions with multiple production and marketing centres, transfers have become a way of castigating individuals, particularly at the managerial level. Madhusudhan, a spinning manager, says,

> If the secretary or another higher authority does not like you, you will be transferred. I have been transferred seven times in the last 30 years. So, you have to be on good terms with them if you want a peaceful life.

Though the working committee is assigned the task of managing the institution, primary producers, who form the bulk of the Khadi community, are often not consulted on vital decisions. Ramanna, a senior salesman in one of the Khadi institutions, says, 'Often we do not even get to know about the working committee meetings. So, it is difficult to give any suggestions.'

Besides, the existing institutional framework is also rigid and it is not easy for outsiders to collaborate with Khadi institutions. Kiran, who runs a boutique store and has a long-standing collaboration with a Khadi institution, sums up his experience:

> It took almost one-and-a-half years to convince and collaborate with a Khadi institution that was about to go defunct. There are so many instances when I had gone from Bengaluru to Hubli with prior appointments. But when I reached the location and called the secretary, he would claim that he was not in town. He was reluctant to meet, to talk or even allow me inside. I was always asked to come to a hotel in front of the bus stand, where we would sit and talk. It took so much of time just to figure out where the institution is and where its production centres are. There were many such challenges. You have to be in constant touch with them. I think many urban designers like me would have exploited them. So, I understand their apprehensions. But I needed to communicate to them somehow that I was not one of them, and to please take me seriously.

Many times, when I order something from Khadi institutions, they accept the order but do not deliver the material even after three months. I go there in person and ask them the reason for the delay. They give all sort of excuses such as festivals, health issues, childbirth and so on. But I work with them without losing my patience. My wife jokes that my patience level has gone up in the last eight years. That is one plus point of working with Khadi institutions! I have stopped wearing a watch now. Why do I even need one when nothing happens on time. Everything is moving at its own pace. So very patiently, I sit and empathise with them. This is how you start. There is no other choice.

My collaboration with the Khadi institution started with one weaver, and later, I added a couple more. Then spinners started coming to me asking why work was being given only to weavers and not to them? So, spinners were also taken on board. Rovings from the CSP were purchased for spinning, we repaired the spinning wheels and looms, got the lighting to work in the shed, and all such facilities were put in place. Now the collaboration is supporting six weavers and 20 spinners.

After such a long and persistent effort of over five years, recently I heard from the secretary that somebody from the KVIC had visited the Khadi institution and had questioned him about the provision of Khadi materials to a private party like me and allowing a monopoly over production. Now the secretary is afraid to continue the collaboration with me. How can Khadi survive with this kind of institutional structure?

Apart from the institutional framework, the scale of the enterprise has become a significant factor in the centralisation of power. The focus of institutions on increasing productivity has encouraged them to expand and operate multiple production sites and sales units. This, in turn, has a centripetal effect on decision making in order to coordinate the increasing operations. However, this has resulted in many problems. The centralisation gives little power to primary producers to participate in the decision-making process, leaving them feeling marginalised and powerless. Due to the increased distance of primary producers from power brought on by the growth in scale, there is less chance for workers to challenge the abuses of power. Often primary producers, being at the bottom of the institutional hierarchy, do not even get to know about the misuse of power. Ramesh, a weaving supervisor, says, 'I agree. The vastness of our institution is a problem. It is like an ocean. If someone catches a fish, no one will get to know.' Similarly, Gopi, a sales manager, avers, 'A small institution will have more control. Small is beautiful.' This resonates with findings by Sale, who points out, 'A small workplace will have no particular difficulty in achieving worker control.'[44[p.237]] It is evident that centralisation has created inefficiencies in the functioning of the institutions. Madhusudhan, a clerk in a Khadi institution states, 'Since ours is a big organisation, it takes at least one week's time just to prepare bills related to wages.' This, in turn, causes delay in dispersing wages for workers. The following conversation between Guruprasad, a weaving supervisor, and Maadamma, an elderly weaver at the production centre of a Khadi institution, shows the impact of scale on the agency of people and the efficiency of the institution:

Maadamma: There is no proper light in the room. I have been asking the master to change the burnt light bulb for the last two months. Since I am old, I cannot see the threads even if it gets a little dark and I cannot weave. Whenever I ask him to replace it, he says he will do it, but still has not kept his word.

Madhusudan: I cannot replace it by myself. It is not like our home. There are higher authorities on me. Once I get permission from them, then I will do it. It is the end of March, and the accounts are being audited. That is why it is taking time. When I told the higher authority, he said that he would send a new bulb. I would have replaced it if I were promised I would be reimbursed the money. So, I cannot do anything right now. Similarly, a few months back, there was no firewood for sizing the yarn. Despite asking many times, nothing happened. Finally, I spent Rs 500 ($6) from my own pocket and got firewood to give work to these women. However, I have still not been reimbursed the money.

Maadamma: Why would higher authorities bother? They get a salary even if they just sit or stand.

The increase in the scale has put enormous pressure on the institution to provide work to a large number of people. But it is the smaller production centres that have a greater chance of offering continuous work. According to Mallamma,

In this centre, we are only 15 spinners. However, that is not the case with Hosahalli centre where there are more than 80 spinners. The organisation there requires more money for raw materials to keep the work going. You cannot give work only to a select few. Hence, if there is a shortage of money, the whole centre will be shut down. However, that is not the case here because we are a small centre.

As Gopinath points out, there has been a 'lack of skill formation over the years' within the Khadi institutions.[13[p.335]] This can be attributed to the scale of purchase orders, particularly of a single kind of material, from wholesale buyers. Such orders have significantly narrowed the skills of Khadi producers and have encouraged Khadi institutions to engage in corrupt practices. For example, the government is one of the significant Khadi purchasers, with many departments, particularly railways, procuring a large volume of Khadi materials to support the sector. Even though it has helped Khadi institutions to some extent, it has resulted in deskilling of the producers because of the demand for a single kind of Khadi material in large scale. Kiran, a designer who is associated with the Khadi sector, states in response to the recent move by the government to advocate Khadi uniforms and combat outfits for the country's paramilitary to support the Khadi sector:

> When will this stop? Producing millions of meters. This is such a scam. The government has already deskilled some of the Khadi institutions in Karnataka by giving them the orders of railways. As a result, many of those institutions have power-looms within their premises to weave vast quantities. They weave lakhs of meters of Khadi on power looms, send them to Erode for chemical dyeing and then to Mumbai. In between, there are numerous inspections and audits. Khadi institutions that have taken the orders have gone bankrupt by just paying bribes to the officials.

In short, the power relations at Khadi institutions are highly centralised, with power concentrated in the hands of the secretary and the decision making largely based on majoritarian resolution. This has led to the pervasive exploitation, corruption, silencing of dissenting voices, nepotism and favouring loyalists. The condition shows that '[c]entralization is the grave of democracy.'[25[p.171]] There is a widespread feeling of powerlessness and a lack of control over their lives among primary producers due to the limited space to participate in decision making. Such a centralisation of power and the failure to enhance the self-rule of individuals has led Khadi institutions to significantly depart from the Swaraj Development Paradigm.

While there is widespread exploitation in the form of red-tape, corruption and disproportionate favours within the Khadi sector in Karnataka, the resistance, unfortunately, is negligible. A large section of the workers fear that any form of resistance would eventually create more problems. It is found that the material conditions of individuals often do not allow them to take up resistance. There is a sense of fear that expulsion from work due to such a protest would eventually put them and their families in distress, so they prefer to remain silent in the face of exploitation. Chinnamma, a spinner, says, 'If we question the supervisor, he will say just work or go home. What can we do? How can we feed ourselves? That is why we do not ask anything.' Similarly, Lakshmana, a supervisor, states, 'If you question the management, you will be transferred and made to suffer in different ways. That is why we do not raise questions.' Such a fear of losing one's job is strongly felt across the sector, even in the KVIC and the KSKVIB. For example, Vineet, a clerk at a KSKVIB district office remarks, 'Working honestly in a government department is not that easy. You know how it works. I do not have to explain.' Similarly, Nayak, a member of the south zone KVIC, states, 'It is difficult to be truthful in our work. There will be a lot of pressure on you from higher authorities and politicians.'

The fear of reprisal is striking not just among individuals but also between institutions. Madan, the secretary of a Khadi institution, remarks, 'We cannot stop corruption in the KSKVIB or the KVIC. If you question them, they will find one or the other mistake in your documents and not release grants. Then the whole institution suffers.' Besides the fear of suffering, people are also afraid of what other people will think about them if they resist, when all others have accepted the oppressive working conditions. For example, Amith, a sales supervisor, says,

> When we participate in the KVIC or the KSKVIB organised exhibitions, there will be fake Khadi stalls. They sell power loom textiles as Khadi for a lower price, and it affects genuine sales. We do not protest because it brings a bad name to the organisation.

However, there are some efforts, albeit not always successful, at resistance by workers. Anitha, a weaver at a Khadi institution, states,

> Once we all came together to protest against the management. We told them that we would not work if our problems remain unresolved and asked them to close down the unit. They assured us that they would do something about it, but nothing happened. Now, people have lost hope. I am not sure how many will turn up if we protest again.

Similarly, sales supervisor Arvind states,

> In a recent exhibition, I fought with the organisers for giving a stall to a power loom textile manufacturer. I said that if they were going to sell their materials, we would not sell ours. By then, press reporters and a district officer had come to the spot. The power loom textile manufacturer was asked to back off. When this happened, other Khadi sellers did not stand by me. Only I ended up having a bad relationship with the organisers.

Mohan, a CSP worker, narrates an unsuccessful effort at resisting against the management:

> Once, through the workers union, we complained about the manager to a south zone member. But nothing happened, since both were on good terms. On the National Geographic channel, see how the lions separate the herd to hunt... In a similar manner, the management employs the British policy of divide and rule against us. They make us suffer until our retirement. Therefore, it is tough to put up any kind of protest.

Resistance is equally hard within the government machinery. Hari, a first division clerk at a district office of the KSKVIB, says,

> It is difficult to work honestly in government jobs. There will be much pressure from politicians. It is like following the direction of the river's flow. Once, I tried to swim against the flow, but eventually, I was made to go with the flow. This is the case in all government departments.

Most importantly, a lack of unity and solidarity among the workers due to the placing of individual self-interest over group interest, indifferent attitudes towards people from other social positions and differences of opinions have reduced their strength and ability to stand up against the more powerful in the sector. Nagananda, a worker at the CSP, states, 'There is no unity among workers. They only think about themselves and are only concerned about their daily wages. That is why we are not in a position to demand or protest as a union.' The same notion is present across different sections of the Khadi sector. The passive nature of Khadi workers to their exploitation leaves the sector far out of alignment with the Swaraj Development Paradigm.

Economy

The KVIC and the KSKVIB

It is evident by now that the Khadi sector is over-regulated by the state through the KVIC and the KSKVIB. Within the evaluated sections of the state machinery, permanent employees are earning anywhere between Rs 25,000 ($316) and 200,000 ($2,525) per month whereas temporary staff earn between Rs 15,000 ($189) and 20,000 ($252) per month. There is a visible spike in salaries as we move towards the top of the bureaucratic hierarchy. The wages are fixed according to pay scales set by the state, with the salaries for the KVIC staff being higher than those of the employees at the KSKVIB. The people associated with the state machinery are the highest earners within the sector. This is not dissimilar to the conditions Kumarappa observed in his day, where 'princely salaries of Government servants' created a 'glamorous attraction to the desk' and were 'responsible for driving all the educated into clerical jobs.'[25[p.146]] Devaraj, a first division clerk at a district Khadi office, says, 'I am a degree holder... My work is not exciting. Yet, I am in this job because I get a good salary and have financial security.' This opinion is widely present among the people employed at the KVIC and the KSKVIB.

The working conditions at the KVIC and the KSKVIB vary according to the workers' positions in the hierarchy, with district offices being small, secluded and non-air conditioned, in contrast to the more commodious and comfortable state and national headquarters. The working hours are from 10 am to 5 pm with a six-day work week. The nature of the work is more intellectual and entails little or no physical work but the space for exercising creativity in this line of work is mostly absent.

Many who are employed in the KVIC and the KSKVIB work at these institutions because of the financial security the job provides rather than a passion for Khadi. Despite the lack of passion, many of them are still content with their jobs. As Mahalakshmi, a district officer at the KSKVIB, states, 'Working in the Khadi sector is a great thing. One has to be fortunate to work here because it is a service to the poor.' There is a strong sense that they are helping destitute people. However, many of them have a sense of superiority because they are associated with the government. Take Rohith, a Khadi officer at the KVIC regional office, who tells me, 'Please do not compare us with weavers or spinners. We fall under the central government.' Most of these employees are satisfied with their income and see no issue with their children following in their footsteps.

However, a majority of the workers at the KVIC and the KSKVIB know little about the history and ideology of Khadi, except for a vague understanding of its connection to Gandhi and the freedom struggle. Many of them believe that Khadi is 'handmade' or 'handspun' cloth and have divergent views on the future of Khadi. According to Manjunath, a second division clerk at one of the district offices of the KSKVIB, 'the Khadi sector will thrive in the future because of the increasing support from the government.' Others, like Gopi, a district KSKVIB officer, hold a contrary opinion. 'Since the younger generation is not coming into the sector, it will die out in the future,' he rues. While these two opinions co-exist, yet another smaller section of workers believes that Khadi will survive in the future, albeit in a different form. Girish, an officer at the KVIC, says 'Modern technologies will be used in the production of Khadi instead of a hand-operated process. It is already happening. The government is encouraging solar spinning and weaving.' Many of the employees at the KVIC and KSKVIB believe that the Khadi sector can be strengthened by asking for increased financial support from the state, paying the incentives in a timely manner to ensure a secure cash flow among Khadi workers, introducing new designs in Khadi fabrics accompanied by more rigorous sales publicity and educating youngsters and the public about Khadi.

The Central Sliver Plant

Even though cotton farming and ginning (the process of separating cotton lint from the seed) constitute the initial phases of the Khadi supply chain, they are deemed as independent of the Khadi sector by the state. This is because these processes not only provide raw material to the Khadi sector but also to the handloom and power loom sectors. As a result, the Khadi supply chain officially starts from the processing of cotton lint. The procurement of raw materials is a difficult task for Khadi institutions because there are few cotton processing units that can furnish them with rovings in a suitable form for hand-spinning machines. Most of the cotton processing plants provide cotton in the form of yarn for power loom and handloom sectors. Since the available cotton processing machinery operates on a large scale that requires enormous investment, independent Khadi institutions are not in a position to run their own cotton processing units. As a result, the state has intervened to resolve the bottleneck by setting up Central Sliver Plants (CSPs) that provide raw material for Khadi institutions. According to Madan, a secretary at a Khadi institution, 'If the CSP was not there, then it would have been challenging for us to procure raw material.'

The CSP converts cotton lint into rovings, which involves sub-processes such as procuring cotton bales, blowing, carding, drawing and slivering. Cotton lint, in the form of bales, is procured through tendering from private firms or from the Cotton Corporation of India. Once the compressed bales are purchased, they are processed in a blow room, where bales are opened, cleaned and mixed to form uniform laps in the form of flat sheets. The laps are fed into carding machines, in which the cotton fibres are disentangled, cleaned, intermixed and aligned to produce a continuous sliver in the form of tape. It is then processed in a draw frame, where slivers are blended and dusted out to form finer slivers. Next, they are fed into roving machines, where the finer slivers are twisted to form long and narrow cotton bundles. These cotton bundles (rovings) are sold to Khadi institutions for further processing. Wages for the workers at the CSP are fixed based on a pay scale set by the state. More than half of the workforce at the CSP comprises permanent employees, who earn an average salary of Rs 30,000 to 40,000 ($378–$505) per month. The rest of the employees work on daily wages and earn an average salary of Rs 8,000 to Rs 12,000 ($101–$151) per month. The unit manager earns the highest salary of Rs 200,000 ($2525) per month. The extreme wage difference between primary workers and the manager shows a perceived superiority of intellectual work over physical work in the sector.

Work conditions at the CSP are very different from those of the KVIC and the KSKVIB. The CSP is a sizeable operation having massive capital investment, which makes it impossible for its workers to own the means of production. The production capacity of the unit that was assessed is about 1 million kilograms of rovings per year but the production targets are fixed every year based on projections of demand. The unit runs throughout the year in three shifts and about a dozen people work in a shift that changes once a week. There is a strict work time where each worker engages with a single process throughout the shift, and they are expected to carry out production without a break. A stark division of labour is present like in any other factory set up, but most of the workers have become familiar with the various production processes involved in the unit, and their work gets reallocated if someone is absent or takes leave. The workers bring food from their homes and a short lunch break is the only leisure time they have in a shift. They work for six days a week and are allowed to take about 70 days of leave per year.

Since the means of production involves automated machines, the use of human energy in the production process at the CSP is limited. Further, there is no space for workers to exert their creative potential at work, which is largely monotonous. This resonates with Kumarappa's claim that 'where need for standardisation brings about centralisation of production, there can be no variegation in the product.'[25[p.170]] Many in the workforce echo the sentiment express by Vignesh, one of the workers, 'The job is boring because there is no change in work. I am working here only because there is a good salary.' Employees' work hours are also profoundly shaped by the pressure of running the machines to meet production targets. A massive investment in the means of production demands that individuals adjust their lives around the operations of the machinery, which are run without interruption to make production economically viable. This has resulted in a situation where workers have become cogs in a wheel and the pace of their lives is primarily controlled by machines. Such work conditions evoke Kumarappa's warning that 'the right place of a machine is an instrument in the hands of man' and that 'when man is turned into a machine-feeder, the whole organisation is up-side-down.'[25[p.15]]

The workers at the CSP have little time for their social lives. According to one worker named Basappa, 'I would like to know more about Khadi but I do not have the time. As you see, I come here to work and go back home for sleep.' The workers work amid cotton dust which is ejected during the processing of cotton. Though a dust absorption mechanism is in place, it is run sporadically. This has had negative implications on the health of several workers, with many facing respiratory ailments. For example, Suresh who works in a blow room, says, 'Salary is not a problem, but health is the major concern. In this cotton dust, you cannot work for more than 15 years. You will ruin your life.' Further, the heat inside the work shed and the enormous noise produced by the machines make the work experience unpleasant. The workers are afraid of approaching higher authorities for a solution and also anxious about the injuries that might occur at the workplace, particularly after an accident where a worker lost his finger while operating a carding machine. Channesh, a worker who operates a sliver making machine, says in hushed tones, 'Supervisors will scold me if they see me talking to you in the middle of the working hours. It's better you come during the night shift. We can talk more freely when the supervisors are not around.'

Most of the workers at the CSP are not cognisant of the implications of their work and have little knowledge about where the raw material is produced. They do, however, possess a vague idea about who buys the manufactured rovings and how they are used further up the supply chain. Most of the workers at the CSP have chosen and continued in this occupation mainly because of a decent salary and the financial security it brings. However, despite having relatively high earnings compared to other primary producers in the sector, a majority of them are not happy. Madhu, a worker, states,

It would be better to have our own business instead of working here. It would be tension-free. There would be more freedom and no orders from higher authorities to follow. However, there would be a risk of losing money. I am still here because it is a government job.

However, many of them feel that they should be compensated better for their work. Hanumantha, a worker, explains, 'The salary should be more if children's education and health expenses are taken into account.' Many workers also grumble that they do not have enough benefits like in the other government departments. According to Hariprasad, another worker, 'We do not have a pension and other benefits like in the railways, despite being a part of the central government.'

The monotony at work, lack of control over their time and unhealthy working conditions at the CSP are the key reasons for their discontent. Nobody desires to see their children working in the positions they have occupied. Ravi, one of the workers, says,

I will not allow my children to work here, not even let them enter the premises. I am fine even if they work as wage labourers but never in this job. As you see, it is so difficult to work in shifts, particularly in the night and in cotton dust.

These workers aspire for their children to find jobs that have a healthier work atmosphere and do not require physical labour as theirs do. In contrast, managers and office staff are generally happy with their work-life and hope to see their children continue in the sector, particularly in high-paid bureaucratic positions. Further, these managers can count on old age pensions, like in other government jobs.

A majority of the workers employed at the CSP have a vague understanding of Khadi in relation to Gandhi and the freedom movement as well. Harsha, a clerk at the CSP, feels that 'People respect Khadi because it was started by Gandhi. It is an inspiration because Khadi freed India from the control of the British.' In contrast, Manjunath, a worker, believes, 'People would have forgotten Gandhi by now. It has not happened yet only because he is on our currency.' According to Rama,

When Gandhi started Khadi, it was highly respected by people. I have heard that many people in our village would not wearing slippers or eat non-vegetarian when they wore Khadi. However, today, Khadi has become *khao khao*. It means bribery and corruption.

Even though there is discontent among workers about the state of contemporary Khadi, some of them are pleased to be a part of the sector. Chaluvaraj, a worker, says, 'I do not know much about Khadi. However, I am happy that I am in the sector that was started by a great person like Gandhi.' Similarly, another worker, Keshava, feels, 'I am proud to be in the Khadi sector because it manufactures the national flag.' Ashok, a supervisor at the CSP, believes that 'Khadi is a service to people. That means service to God.'

Khadi Institutions

The work at Khadi institutions involves spinning, dyeing, weaving, block-printing, tailoring and marketing. However, the production activities vary from institution to institution according to their capacity, convenience and local circumstances. The wages for the workforce at Khadi institutions are set according to the previously recommended production cost chart and not according to the revised pricing structure advised by the KVIC based on the ability of Khadi institutions to sell products in the competitive market. These institutions follow the prescribed production cost chart, because doing so is stipulated as part of the financial assistance provided by the state, particularly Modified Marketing Development Assistance (MMDA) scheme. However, such a fixing of wages is inadequate because it employs uniform costing across the country while not capturing the real production costs as well as other market variables that vary by location and time of the year.[28[p.6,7]]

Even though most of the Khadi institutions buy roving from the CSP, there are still a few institutions that make their own rovings on a small scale. However, the units supply only a small portion of the operation's total consumption. The roving-making process in these units is similar to the CSP, and the production capacity is around 2,00,000 kg of rovings per year. Usually, a dozen people are employed in such units and earn salaries between Rs 5,000 ($63) and Rs 8,000 ($101) per month.

Spinning is the next process in the production chain. Hand spinning on new model spinning machines is the key activity that differentiates the Khadi sector from the handloom sector, which uses machine-spun yarn. It is a process that converts rovings into yarn in the form of hanks, which are 1,000 meters in length. Although the count (thickness) of the produced yarn varies from coarse to fine, the medium 33 count yarn is the most commonly produced one. Even though the wages are based on production, there are no fixed targets for workers. The average production capacity of each worker on the most common eight spindle spinning machine is three hanks per hour. In a day, workers produce an average of 15 to 25 hanks, depending upon their hours of work. They are paid Rs 5 ($0.06) per hank as wages, while Rs 3 ($0.03) per hank is paid as an incentive by the KSKVIB, up to a maximum of 1,500 hanks per person per year. On an average, a spinner earns about Rs 2,000 ($25) to Rs 3,000 ($38) per month.

The next process in Khadi production after spinning is the sizing of yarn. The quality of handspun yarn varies due to the pace of spinning by individual spinners. It becomes necessary to pre-treat or size the handspun yarn with starch to give it strength and reduce yarn breakage during the weaving process. The sizing process is carried out by a few people, mostly as part-time work. Typically, about 1,000 hanks are sized in a day, which also involves treating and sun drying the hanks. People who do sizing are paid based on a piece rate or salary depending on the local circumstances, and they usually earn about Rs 1,000 ($12) to Rs 2,000 ($25) a month.

The sized yarns are winded into bobbins using bobbin winders. This process is mostly carried out by older women, since it does not involve hard physical labour. A person, on an average, winds about 50 to 80 hanks per day and their wages are based on a piece rate, which is typically around Rs 1.5 ($0.01) to Rs 2 ($0.02) per hank. A bobbin winder earns an average of Rs 1,500 ($19) to Rs 2,500 ($32) per month. Winded bobbins are converted into a warp on a warping machine to produce 100 to 150 meters of warp. It usually takes about a day and a half or two to prepare a warp by a single person. The warpers are also paid in the form of a piece rate based on local circumstances, and earn about Rs 4,000 ($51) to Rs 6,000 ($76) per month.

The prepared warps are then set on the looms. It takes about a day for a weaver to connect each thread of the new warp to the end of the old warp. Then the hanks are winded into pirns (a rod onto which weft thread is wound for use in weaving) on the pirn winding machines and used in the shuttles during the weaving process. The weaving takes place mainly on frame looms, which are an improved version of the traditional pit looms. The average production capacity of a weaver is about one meter per hour, and about six to eight meters a day. The weavers are paid based on a piece rate that is typically about Rs 20 ($0.25) per meter. An additional Rs 7 ($0.08) per meter is also paid as an incentive by the KSKVIB for a maximum of 700 meters per person per year. On an average, a weaver earns about Rs 2,500 ($32) to Rs 4,000 ($51) per month.

The dyeing, block printing and tailoring works are mostly outsourced by Khadi institutions. However, one institution that was studied had a defunct chemical dying unit, small but active chemical block printing unit as well as a tailoring unit. The dyeing unit had been closed for the last three years due to a malfunctioning boiler. The workers who used to work in the dyeing unit are now involved in other production-related activities. They earn about Rs 5,000 ($63) to Rs 8,000 ($101) per month in the form of a salary. The workers at the block printing unit mainly print 'Ashoka chakra' on the national flag and are paid about Rs 6,500 ($82) salary per month. The tailoring unit predominantly stitches the national flag of various sizes and the tailors are paid based on piece rates from Rs 9 ($0.11) to Rs 300 ($4) depending upon the size of the flag, and earn an average of Rs 3,000 ($38) to 5,000 ($63) per month.

The final process of marketing the finished Khadi products is carried out by both Khadi producing institutions as well as certified private entities. The Khadi institutions use physical stores and state-organised Khadi exhibitions as key marketing channels. The workers involved in marketing are paid monthly salaries of about Rs 5,000 ($63) to 15,000 ($189) per month depending on their experience whereas the secretaries of Khadi institutions earn about Rs 7,000 ($88) to Rs 15,000 ($189) a month.

There stark income inequality is visible in the existing Khadi supply chain. Though primary producers form the largest group, they earn the lowest income. The salary of employees at the KVIC and the KSKVIB, on average, is seven times more than the primary producers. It demonstrates that those who are meant to support the primary producers have themselves become the major beneficiaries in the Khadi sector. As Gopinath suggests, 'it appears that KVIC and its programme-implementing institutions have taken up Khadi work largely to avail of the other financial benefits provided by the Government.'[13[p.322]])

The workforce at the Khadi institutions that were evaluated consisted mainly of spinners, followed by weavers. The other salaried employees, particularly supervisors and managers, are the smallest segment of the Khadi workforce but earn significantly more than all the other workers employed. A similar observation has also been made by Debashish Mahalanabish and others, who observe that, on average, the workforce at a Khadi institution contains 78% spinners, 13% weavers and 9% salaried employees, whereas their earning shares are 28%, 32% and

40%, respectively.[45[p.203]] This evidences the highly unequal income distribution present within Khadi institutions.

The employees at the Khadi institutions largely carry out their work at dedicated spaces. However, there are cases of workers carrying out activities from their homes, especially spinning and weaving, depending upon the local conditions. The dedicated spaces are normally old work sheds/buildings with broken windows, cracked doors, improper roofing (mostly made of asbestos), poor ventilation, no electricity and no toilets—all the standard features of a place in shambles. There is a strong discontent among employees about these workspaces. Sujathamma, a bobbin winder at a Khadi institution, says ironically, 'In summer, we do not need to take a shower because every day we take a sweat bath while working here.' A young weaver, Ragini, bemoans, 'Forget toilets, we do not even have water facilities here.' Jayamma, a middle-aged spinner, says, 'We have been asking the supervisor to repair the roof for the last eight years. Still, it has not been fixed.'

Women form the primary workforce at Khadi institutions, and they typically start their work after finishing their household responsibilities. Workhour flexibility is a key feature of the production process. However, workers are highly dependent on unit managers who provide them with raw materials. This power relation pressures workers to avoid questioning their managers. Any grievance can lead to delays in the provision of raw materials or, worst case scenario, the dismissal of the worker.

Since Khadi work is mainly a group activity, the production units of Khadi institutions are important places of social interaction. Workers usually talk to each other on topics ranging from family issues to state politics. They often leave their work whenever they want, except for those occupied in roving-making and other salary-based occupations. The reasons for such breaks are diverse, such as unexpected visitors to their homes, fetching water on days it is available from the public water system, feeding their children and other members of the family, overseeing livestock, collecting rations and so on. Workers, especially within the old age group, bring lunch to the workplace, whereas others go back to their homes. The lunch break varies from half an hour to a few hours depending on their other engagements. They leave their workplace who do shopping mostly on those times around 5 in the evening.

The stores of Khadi institutions generally open six days a week from 10 am to 5 pm. Since the outlets normally remain shut during prime shopping times such as late evenings and on Sundays, they fail to cater to large section of consumers. The abysmal display of products and lack of enthusiasm among salespeople to showcase the available products to customers are commonly noticed. Besides, poor language skills and a woeful lack of confidence in convincing customers among a significant section of Khadi salespeople is a deterrent to effective marketing. When they were asked about how they attempt to persuade consumers to buy Khadi, their responses were limited. For most of them, making a successful sale rests upon the argument that Khadi is good for one's health and that it is comfortable to wear. For example, Mukunda, a salesman, says, 'Khadi is comfortable because it will keep you warm when it is cold outside and keep you cool when it is hot outside.' According to Kalpana, a saleswoman, 'People should buy Khadi because it is good for health, since it absorbs sweat and keeps the skin clean.' Their knowledge is often limited and many do not know the difference between Khadi and handloom fabrics. Similar observations have also been made by Goel and Jain[34[p.101]], who claim there is a lack of 'professional training' and 'low motivation towards selling the Khadi' among salesmen.

The people involved in marketing often grumble about the price of Khadi products. For example, Ravi, a salesman, states, 'Just as I prefer less expensive products, customers too look for cheaper products. That is why the government should make sure that Khadi can be sold at the same price as power loom products.' Besides, there is little emphasis on the promotion of their products by the Khadi institutions. As identified by scholars Nair and Dhanuraj, the Khadi stores are largely dependent on 'outdated marketing techniques such as heavily relying on print advertising.'[31[p.2]] The sales are significantly higher during the 35% discount period that extends over 154 days of the year. At other times, a 15% discount is given to the customers. However, according to the evaluation report of the Planning Commission, the 'average unintended stock build-up is around 35% of the annual production, and for small units, it is as high as 80%.'[33[p.7]] The pile up of stock due to such poor sales is one of the main factors for many Khadi institutions becoming defunct.

Often, since workers are also members of the Khadi institution, an ownership of the means of production lays indirectly with them. However, in reality, the institutional framework has not created this sense of ownership. The means of production primarily relies largely on human energy, except in the cotton processing stages of blowing to roving. The cotton processing and spinning work are monotonous whereas weaving gives greater scope for workers to exercise some artistic potential. The defunct chemical dyeing unit that was observed mainly involved automated processes, and it could be presumed that the space for exercising creativity at the unit was considerably low.

The block printing unit that was evaluated relied on human energy as well as electricity in the production process. Even though there is abundant space for exercising artistry in block printing, the work at the unit appeared to be dull and dreary, largely because the units tend to manufacture single products, like national flags, throughout the year. The tailoring unit that was investigated mostly ran on electricity. While tailoring too offers scope for ingenuity, the work at the unit was, similar to the printing process, mechanical due to the production of a single product throughout the year. The marketing process relies almost entirely on human energy, and it offers a creative space for workers to engage with customers and, potentially, educate them about Khadi.

The overall working conditions at Khadi institutions are not always pleasant, and they can be demoralising for some workers. As a report from the Planning Commission itself summarises:

> the quantity and quality of employment are not satisfactory at present, because of low and shrinking production base. Factors, such as unintended stock build-up, constraints to input availability, capital of institutions/units getting locked up for years, non-availability of improved technologies and repair facilities, outmoded product mix etc. have all contributed in different degrees to the present sorry state of affairs.[33[p.9]]

There is greater understanding among workers at the Khadi institutions about the sourcing of the raw material and what happens further up the supply chain. However, there is no clear understanding of the social conditions under which the raw materials are produced. There is also little awareness of the environmental impact of their work. Many workers prefer working in the Khadi sector because of the flexible hours and because it provides space for social interaction. A sizeable number of Khadi producers, however, are discontent with their work due to the low wages, as summed up by Bhagirathi, a spinner: 'We earn a few thousand rupees a month, which is not at all enough to sustain our family.'

Many primary producers at Khadi institutions aspire for an income of about Rs 5,000 ($63) to 10,000 ($126) per month. There is a general feeling among managers and salespeople that they should earn at least Rs 10,000 ($126) to 15,000 ($189) per month, whereas most secretaries believe they should get at least around Rs 15,000 ($189) to 30,000 ($379) per month. What is evident is that most of the workers have not taken up their positions out of choice, and they do not wish for their children to follow the same occupational path. Pallavi, a weaver, laments:

> Work, work, work! No energy left in our bodies. I am not able to sustain myself in this work. How could I ask my children or others

to come and join? The work will die along with us. Nobody will do this job once we leave.

Likewise, Guru Prasanna, a supervisor at a Khadi institution, says, 'I would like my son to be an officer. This work is enough for me.' The same perspective is prevalent among Khadi workers. But there are some instances where workers seem content in their roles. Take Shwetha, a tailor, for instance. She says, 'I am happy in the work because I am serving the country by making the national flag. I am fortunate that I am doing this work. Not everybody gets the opportunity to do the work that I am doing.' Such a notion tied to patriotism is especially present among those who are involved in the manufacture of the national flag.

Yet, many of the workers at the Khadi institutions wish for health benefits, scholarships for their children's education, pensions and support to build their houses. According to Rekha, a weaver,

> We need a pension. See that 80-year-old lady over there who is winding the bobbins. Nobody is there to look after her. She has worked for so many decades in this Khadi institution. Somebody has to support her in her old age.

A majority of the workers at Khadi institutions do not know what Khadi is. For many of them, it represents 'cotton,' 'cotton cloth,' 'handspun cloth' and 'handwoven cloth.' However, they have little idea about Khadi's emphasis on the importance of human energy. As Ratnamma, a weaver says, 'There is nobody to tell us about Khadi. I do not know why Khadi has to be produced through a hand-operated process.' Workers are also not aware of the Khadi ideology. They make loose connections with Gandhi and the freedom struggle to some extent. They all hold Gandhi in high regard, even if they do not know much about him. For example, Laxmi, a 70-old spinner, says, 'There is nobody to help us. We remember Gandhi thaata (Kannada for grandfather) every day and get on with our lives. Gandhi is the one who worked honestly.'

There is widespread belief among people at Khadi institutions that the sector can be strengthened by increasing the financial support from the state, making sure that Khadi workers earn living wages and get continuous work throughout the year, bringing new technologies like solar-powered spinning machines and looms, diversifying Khadi production, improving designs and publicising Khadi products.

Exchange, Consumption, Disposal of Khadi

The exchange between producers and consumers in the Khadi sector is impersonal. Like for most goods, money is the medium of exchange. This contributes to the apparent disconnect between primary producers and consumers, since the production takes place mostly in rural areas, removed from the urban spaces where they are often consumed. Therefore, the morality of consumers remains limited since they do not see the production processes. According to Ramesh, a consumer who was interviewed, 'I do not know who produces these materials. I buy Khadi because it is comfortable and it is a product of our country. However, it is a little expensive.' This kind of a clinical exchange without knowing about the producers or their working conditions seems pervasive among Khadi consumers.

Khadi is overwhelmingly produced for the market and less for self-consumption by its producers. There is no conception or aspiration for greater self-sufficiency among its producers, as was the thought behind the Swaraj Development Paradigm. The share of Khadi consumed by producers is negligible when compared to the consumption by non-producers. Despite having the capacity to afford Khadi, employees at the KVIC and the KSKVIB who wear cotton Khadi on an everyday basis are in the minority. Even amongst Khadi workers, there is a general perception that it is expensive compared to other materials. Additionally, they are commonly of the opinion that it requires extra care. As Kiran, a clerk at the KSKVIB, says, 'Khadi requires maintenance like starching and ironing. That is why I do not wear it regularly.' Many people at the KVIC and the KSKVIB, though, wear Khadi because it is mandatory for employees.

People at the CSP are in the second highest paying positions in the sector. The consumption habits among them are similar to the people at the KVIC and the KSKVIB. Most of them believe that Khadi materials do not have the suitable elasticity and strength to endure their working conditions. However, some of them have bought Khadi for special occasions mainly because as Ramanuja, one of the workers, says, 'Khadi absorbs sweat. Therefore, it is more comfortable.'

Although most workers at Khadi institutions would like to wear what they have produced, they find it unaffordable. According to Nalini, a spinner, 'We cannot buy Khadi from the money that we earn by doing this work.' Similarly, Suchitra, a weaver, states, 'I would like to wear what I make, but it is costly. I buy two sarees for Rs 500 ($6) in the market. Whereas, the cost of one Khadi saree that I weave is a few thousand rupees.' On average, the finished Khadi goods are three times more expensive than the power loom materials that they usually wear.

Apart from affordability, design is another factor that makes workers value other materials over their own produce. Vimala, a spinner, says, 'I prefer non-Khadi cloth because they have better designs, colours and finishing.' However, some of them do own a few pairs of Khadi clothes in their collection, mainly due to the payment of bonuses received in the form of Khadi materials. These tend to be worn mostly on special occasions or for functions that are hosted by their institutions as well as for the visits from higher authorities and politicians to their workplaces.

In contrast, however, many salespeople in shops are generally found wearing Khadi. As Manjunath, a salesman says, 'I wear Khadi regularly. If I do not wear it, then who else will?' Even though such a sentiment is present among salesmen, most prefer polyester Khadi over cotton Khadi. Vishwanath, another salesman, explains, 'Cotton Khadi requires ironing but polyester Khadi does not. More importantly, the finishing and texture of the latter are smooth compared to the former. That is why I prefer polyester Khadi.'

Big cities like Bengaluru are the largest consumption centres of Khadi products. It is because the average income of people settled in urban areas is four times higher than that of those settled in rural areas.[46[p.4]] Therefore, Khadi, which is generally more expensive than other textiles, is largely dependent on an urban consumer base. These consumers, though, are not very aware of the ideology underpinning Khadi production and think little about the implications of their purchase on society and the environment at large. As Kumarappa says, '[o]ften buyers are only concerned with satisfying their own requirements as near as possible and as cheaply as they can.'[25[p.77]] In spite of the low awareness among consumers, they purchase Khadi because of various other reasons.

Regular Khadi wearers tend to buy Khadi because of its perceived comfort. Rani, who works in a government department, notes that 'Khadi is more comfortable because it has good aeration and absorbs sweat. So, I prefer to buy it.' As opposed to this, some consumers prefer unstitched Khadi materials because of the discomfort of Khadi garments. Akash, a police officer, says,

> I wear branded cotton shirts. They are so comfortable, and there will not be a change even in one stitch. However, Khadi materials often shrink and I cannot wear them without ironing. That is why I prefer only unstitched Khadi materials, like towels.

A small section of elderly people who lived through the era of the Indian freedom movement regularly buy Khadi for its historical value. Alok, a retired bank manager, says, 'It is the fabric that got us freedom. Hence, I buy Khadi.' Another important consumer segment is politicians. According to Malini, a saleswoman, 'Politicians buy Khadi mostly of white colour.' It would appear that they do so to represent themselves as a part of the nationalist tradition and to associate themselves with India's freedom fighters.

Another consumer segment is made up of those who operate from a strong sense of nationalism. They buy Khadi with the assumption that it will contribute to transforming India into a powerful nation since it is produced within the country. Varsha, a lecturer, states, 'I buy Khadi because it strengthens the national economy.' This line of reasoning could be attributed to the parochial nationalism promoted by the state in recent years through glitzy campaigns run under the banner of 'Make in India.' As Venu Madhav Govindu points out, nationalist consumption has limited benefits for the poor as it tends to support mainly big businesses and foreign investments.[47]

A new and growing segment of Khadi consumers is found among the younger generation who are more concerned about the disadvantaged sections of the society as well as the environment. As asserted by Sanjay K Jain and Gurmeet Kaur, there is a greater tendency among the relatively young, particularly those belonging to the 18–35 year demographic, to shop for socio-ecologically responsible products.[48[p.134]]

Despite it all, there is a certain level of dissatisfaction present among Khadi consumers. Many feel that there is a lack of new collections and are unhappy with the experience of shopping at Khadi outlets, particularly those belonging to Khadi institutions. Vimala, who works as a schoolteacher, observes,

> First of all, there is a lack of collections at Khadi stores. Further, there is a difference between coming here and going to the other stores. Here, they do not persuade us to buy. Salespeople are normally reluctant and we ourselves have to push them to show us different materials.

A similar point is raised by Nitish Goel and Kshitij Jain, who suggest that the 'uneven quality and limited design patterns' at the existing Khadi stores discourage customers from purchasing Khadi products.[34[pp.101–2]]

Further, there is a general perception that the fitting of Khadi garments is not up to the mark. Shekhar, a consumer who works in a bank, observes 'The stitching and design of Khadi materials are not good. Normally, Khadi garments do not fit you. Instead, you need to find ways to fit into the garments.' Most importantly, many consumers think that Khadi clothes are plain and unattractive. Paramesh, who works in a software company, says,

> I used to wear Khadi in my college days. When I started going for a job, I stopped because I felt odd among my colleagues. Also, my wife points out that the designs of these Khadi outfits do not flatter me. Hence I just buy Khadi bedsheets.

A similar observation is also made by Debashish Mahalanabish and others that 'customers become dissatisfied with poor quality of garments, lack of having design value, variety in products etc.'[45[p.204]]

The life span of Khadi materials, though, is relatively longer as it is only occasionally used by most consumers. Sushma, a bank manager, states, 'I wear Khadi once in a while. So, I do not buy it regularly.' Since Khadi materials are made out of uneven yarn quality and have irregular knitting, they demand smooth hand wash and drying under shade in order to maintain their good condition. Since many of the urban Khadi consumers use washing machines and electric dryers, the materials deteriorate more quickly. There is scant awareness among consumers of the social and ecological impact of the disposal of Khadi. For instance, Akshatha, a consumer who works in a college, says, 'I do not have any idea what happens to the used Khadi garments once I throw them away.' There is little effort on the part of the consumers to upcycle used Khadi materials. Such an appalling lack of attention among consumers to the implications of their Khadi purchases on the lives of producers and the impact of their disposal on the society and the environment, make the consumption and disposal stages of the existing Khadi sector inconsistent with the Swaraj Development Paradigm.

Notes

a Cultural memory represents 'historical consciousness' that provides 'diachronic identity' for people in the present. It is referred to as memory because it forgets what lies outside of the horizon of the relevant. It entails 'mythical history' where 'distinction between myth and history vanishes.' Further, it involves 'events from absolute past' from the 'mythical primordial time' spanning over the last 3,000 years. The cultural memory mediates from generation to generation through 'symbols' in the form of structures, texts, rituals, icons, performance of various kinds, classical or other formalised languages[1[pp.109–18]].

b *Dalits* are the members of an outcaste group in India formerly known as untouchables. Currently they form 19.5% of the total population, and are the largest caste entity in Karnataka.[4]

c *Kuruba* is one of the major caste groups in Karnataka, and forms 7% of the total population.[4] Shepherding is their traditional occupation.

d *Vokkaliga* is another major caste group in Karnataka, forming 14% of the total population.[4] They are largely associated with farming activity and tend to own land.

e The Below Poverty Line (BPL) category is a benchmark used by the Government of India to indicate economic disadvantage and to identify people in need of state aid. In the state of Karnataka, it is identified based on four parameters, including: a person who owns not more than 3 acres of land; a person who does not own a four-wheeler apart from having vehicle for livelihood; a person who does not own more than 10 square and 12 squares of property in urban or town spaces; a person who does not pay income tax, service tax, professional tax and working in any government organization, corporations, aided institutions or deemed institutions; and a person from a family having annual income not more than Rs 120,000.[26]

f The reservation is a system formulated by the Government of India to provide opportunities for disadvantaged groups in legislature, government jobs and higher education. Such groups are divided into the historically disadvantaged groups Scheduled Castes (SC) and Scheduled Tribes (ST); educationally and socially disadvantaged groups such as Other Backward Classes (OBC); and the economically weaker section of society as General (GEN).

g Roving is the long bundle of cotton fibres. It is the raw material for hand spinning.

h *Lingayat* is a sect that emphasises theistic devotion to the God Shiva. They are the followers of Basaveshwara, a 12th century South Indian social reformer-philosopher-poet who rejected discrimination based on caste and gender and defied the pre-eminence of Vedic rituals.[42] Today, the sect is considered as a part of Hinduism by the state but there is a long-pending demand from its followers to recognise it as a separate religion. At present, they form 17% of Karnataka's total population.[43]

References

1 Assmann J. Communicative and cultural memory. In: Erll A, Nünning A, editors. *Cultural memory studies: An international and interdisciplinary handbook* (pp. 109–18). Berlin: Walter de Gruyter; 2008.

2 Assmann J, Livingstone R. *Religion and cultural memory: Ten studies.* California: Stanford University Press; 2006.

3 Kumarappa JC. *Non-violent economy and world peace.* Wardha: Akhil Bharat Serva Seva Sangh; 1955.

4 Satish DP. Dalits, Muslims outnumber Lingayats and Vokkaligas in Karnataka? 'Caste Census' stumps Siddaramaiah Govt. *News18* [Internet]. 2018 [cited 2020 Aug 18]. Available from: https://www.news18.com/news/politics/dalits-muslims-outnumber-lingayats-and-vokkaligas-in-karnataka-caste-census-stumps-siddaramaiah-govt-1689531.html

5 Chacko PS, Prashar S, Ramanathan HN. Assessing the relationship between materialism and conspicuous consumption: Validation in the Indian context. *Asian Academy of Management Journal.* 2018;23(2):143–59.

6 Manchanda R, Abidi N, Mishra JK. Assessing materialism in Indian urban youth. *Management.* 2015;20(2):181–203.

7 Berman R. *Advertising and social change.* Beverly Hills: SAGE Publications; 1981.

8 Neve M, Trivedi R. Materialism and media usage: To study the role of media in increasing materialism among youths with special reference to social media exposure. *International Journal of Advanced Science and Technology.* 2020;29(8):2431–6.

9 Sandhu N. Television advertisements and consumerism: Implications for financial health of viewers. *SCMS Journal of Indian Management.* 2017;14(4):112–20.

10 Sinha D. *Consumer India: Inside the Indian mind and wallet.* Hoboken, NJ: John Wiley & Sons Ltd; 2011.

11 Kumarappa JC. *Economy of permanence.* Wardha, India: All India Village Industries Association; 1949.

12 KVIC. Annual report: 2018–19. Government of India; 2019.

13 Gopinath P. Wages, working conditions and socio-economic mobility of spinners and weavers in the unorganised Khadi industry: Findings from a survey in India. *The Indian Journal of Labour Economics.* 2010;53(2):305–38.

14 National Crime Records Bureau. Crime in India: 2018 [Internet]. New Delhi: Ministry of Home Affairs, Government of India; 2019. Available from: https://ncrb.gov.in/sites/default/files/Crime%20in%20India%20 2018%20-%20Volume%201.pdf

15 Dhillon M, Bakaya S. Street harassment: A qualitative study of the experiences of young women in Delhi. *SAGE Open.* 2014;4(3). https://doi.org/10.1177/2158244014543786.

16 Deshpande RS. Agrarian transition and farmers' distress in Karnataka. In: Reddy DN, Mishra S, editors. *Agrarian crisis in India* (pp. 199–229). Oxford: Oxford University Press; 2010.

17 Vasavi AR. Suicides and the making of India's agrarian distress. *South African Review of Sociology.* 2009;40(1):94–108.

18 Deshetti MB, Teggi MY. Socio economic profile and constraints faced by dairy farmers in Vijayapur and Bagalakote districts of Karnataka. *Research Journal of Agricultural Sciences.* 2017;8(4):963–6.

19 Radder SK, Bhanj SK. Perceptions of Dairy Farmers of Gadag district in northwestern part of Karnataka state, India regarding Clean Milk Production. *Veterinary World.* 2011;4(2):79–81.

20 The Dairy Working Group of the Food Sovereignty Alliance. *The milk crisis in India: The story behind the numbers.* Coventry: The Centre for Agroecology, Water and Resilience; 2017.

21 Vasavi AR. *Harbingers of rain: Land and life in South Asia.* Bangalore: Oxford University Press; 1998.

22 Government of Karnataka. Education in Karnataka state, 2011–12: A state-level, district-wise analytical report [Internet]. 2012. Available from: http://ssakarnataka.gov.in/pdfs/data/2011-12_Analytical_Report.pdf

23 Government of India. All India survey on higher education, 2018–19 [Internet]. Ministry of Human Resource Development; 2019. Available from: http://aishe.nic.in/aishe/viewDocument.action?documentId=262

24 Government of Karnataka. School education in Karnataka, 2018–19 [Internet]. 2019. Available from: http://www.schooleducation.kar.nic.in/databank/GoKReport1819Final_230919.pdf

25 Kumarappa JC. *Why the village movement?* Wardha, India: All India Village Industries Association; 1936.

26 Moudgal S. Karnataka govt changes rules for BPL card holders | Bengaluru News—Times of India. The Times of India [Internet]. 2016 [cited 2020 Mar 11]. Available from: https://timesofindia.indiatimes.com/city/bengaluru/Karnataka-govt-changes-rules-for-BPL-card-holders/articleshow/53638642.cms

27 Lambert AJ, Scherer LN, Rogers C, Jacoby L. How does collective memory create a sense of the collective? In: Boyer P, Wertsch JV, editors. *Memory in mind and culture* (pp. 194–217). Cambridge: Cambridge University Press; 2009.

28 Dhanuraj D, Nair L, Varghese JP. *How to revive the Khadi sector—An evaluation with special focus on Khadi act.* Kochi: Centre for Public Policy Research; 2018.

29 Prasad CS. *Exploring Gandhian science: A case study of the Khadi Movement* [Unpublished]. [New Delhi]: Indian Institute of Technology; 2001.

30 Ray S. Vicious circle of impoverisation: Woollen khadi institutions of Rajasthan. *Economic and Political Weekly.* 1998;33(14):788–92.

31 Nair LR, Dhanuraj D. *Evaluation of government interventions in Khadi Sector.* Kochi: Centre for Public Policy Research; 2016.

32 Deshpande N. Hanging by a thread. *Down to Earth.* 2012 May 31.

33 Planning Commission. *Evaluation study on khadi and village industries programme.* New Delhi: Government of India; 2001.

34 Goel N, Jain K. Revival of Khadi—An analysis of the state of khadi in India with supply and demand side problems. *Innovative Journal of Business and Management.* 2015;4(5):100–3.

35 Quah JST. Curbing corruption in India: An impossible dream? *Asian Journal of Political Science.* 2008;16(3):240–59.

36 Transparency International. Corruption Perceptions Index [Internet]. Transparency.org. 2019 [cited 2020 Jul 18]. Available from: https://www.transparency.org/en/cpi/2019/results

37 Gupta A. Changing forms of corruption in India. *Modern Asian Studies.* 2017;51(6):1862–90.

38 Rohini S. Whither khadi? *Economic and Political Weekly.* 2009;44(13):12–15.

39 Dangi BM, Bhise AR. Cotton dust exposure: Analysis of pulmonary function and respiratory symptoms. *Lung India.* 2017;34(2):144–9.

40 Wang XR, Zhang HX, Sun BX, Dai HL, Hang JQ, Eisen EA, et al. A 20-year follow-up study on chronic respiratory effects of exposure to cotton dust. *European Respiratory Journal.* 2005;26(5):881–6.

41 KVIC. Memorandum of institution [Internet]. 2019 [cited 2019 Aug 29]. Available from: http://www.kvic.org.in/kvicres/PDF/Memorandum%20and%20Bylaws_for_Institutions_ENGLISH.pdf

42 Lankesh G. Making Sense of the Lingayat vs Veerashaiva Debate. *The Wire* [Internet]. 2017 Aug 5 [cited 2020 Apr 21]; Available from: https://thewire.in/history/karnataka-lingayat-veerashaive-debate

43 Majumdar N. Who are Lingayats, Veerashaivas, and why they matter in Karnataka polls. *The Print* [Internet]. 2018 Mar 20 [cited 2020 Apr 21]; Available from: https://theprint.in/theprint-essential/who-are-lingayats-veerashaivas-and-why-they-matter-in-karnataka-polls/43421/

44 Sale K. *Human scale revisited: A new look at the classic case for a decentralist future.* Vermont: Chelsea Green Publishing; 2017.
45 Mahalanabish D, Bhattacharya P, Choudhuri PK. A review of khadi fabrics in India. *Journal of the Textile Association.* 2018;79(3):198–206.
46 Das D, Pathak M. The growing rural-urban disparity in India: Some issues. *International Journal of Advancements in Research & Technology.* 2012;1(5):145–51.
47 Govindu VM. Why 'Make For India' Matters as Much as 'Make in India'. *The Wire* [Internet]. 2015 Oct 2; Available from: https://thewire.in/economy/why-make-for-india-matters-as-much-as-make-in-india
48 Jain SK, Kaur G. Role of socio-demographics in segmenting and profiling green consumers: An exploratory study of consumers in India. *Journal of International Consumer Marketing.* 2006;18(3):107–46.

5 Development of Khadi Sector

A Way Forward

In this chapter, I would like to discuss the possible measures that can be taken to transform the Khadi sector closer to the Swaraj Development Vision. The interpretive analysis of the Khadi sector from Chapter 4 as well as other appropriate contemporary initiatives are used as a springboard to offer such potential steps, thereby representing the pragmatic fold of the swaraj development approach discussed in Chapter 1. Although the possible interventions are discussed under different sections namely morality, politics and economy, it is necessary to be aware that they are all interconnected.

Morality

Transforming the morality present within the Khadi community in accordance with the morality of the Swaraj Development Paradigm requires a shift in the cosmological vision of Khadi community. Since their worldview is shaped by cultural memory, rooted in religious texts and symbols, it is essential to engage with it to bring about a desired change. The Khadi community derives practical moral lessons from the narrative tales of the actions of divine providence. Therefore, an 'exegetical exercise' would entail an 'impassionate [re]imagination' of mythology to 'make texts and symbols signify the desired meaning.'[1[p.41]] Such an act of imagination is feasible within the cultural memory because it does not hold a clear distinction between mythology and history. Such an engagement with the cultural memory requires a combination of questioning its defective elements, retaining its sensible aspects and innovating existing materials by employing creative interpretations. It helps to bring transformation in the community by delving into what historian Dharampal refers to as the attitude and attributes of peoples' *chitta* (mind) and sense of *kala* (time).[2[p.149]] Further, such

DOI: 10.4324/9781003353096-8

engagement protects people from the humiliation of seeing their ways being disdained during the process of transformation.

For example, as an apostle of non-violence, Gandhi's radically different interpretation of *Bhagavat Gita*, one of the celestial texts of Hinduism is contrary to the traditional perceptions of Gita as 'transcendence from the world' and a 'call to duty through violence.'[3[p.58]] Through his reading, he elevated the conception of non-violence, which was not a defining element of Hinduism, to a position of central importance within the fold of public consciousness during the time of the independence movement.

Similar is the adaptation of cultural memory during the Chipko movement, the well-known non-violent struggle for forest conservation in the 1970s at the foothills of the Himalayas. The movement utilised locally popular mythological stories, particularly the *Bhagavata Purana*, known also as *Shrimad Bhagavatam*, that contains tales of the adventurous life of Lord Krishna in the forest of Vrindavan as well as his love for nature and its resplendent beauty. These stories were recited during the demonstrations to save the Himalayan forests and acted as cultural resources to reflect upon the moral significance of the forests. Such a creative interpretation of religious stories became one of the most important means of gathering support for the Chipko movement and a way of arousing common humanity to bring the intended social transformation.[4[pp.104–8]]

Even though such engagements are rare in contemporary times, a recent effort on this front is the interpretation of *Ramayana*, one of the epics of Hinduism, by Prasanna, a well-known theatre director and an advocate of handmades in Karnataka. In his book *Moola Ramayana* ("The Original Ramayana"), Prasanna argues that the epic is not merely a story of Lord Rama and his wife Sita, as widely believed. Instead, he suggests, in its original meaning, it advocates a civilisational vision for humanity based on the harmonious relationship between nature and humans while placing physical work at its centre.[5,6] This interpretation, in a subtle way, has brought the discussion about civilisational crisis into contemporary public consciousness in Karnataka.

Apart from the creative engagement with the cultural memory, exposure to an understanding of the natural world helps individuals realise the intricate connections between the self and other beings in the cosmos.[7–11] Recognising the contribution of other beings towards the existence of the self through such exercises encourages an individual to lead a life in accordance with the Natural Order. It helps to expand a person's empathy while lessening the demands of the egoistic self. This enhances the commitment to the morality of greatest good of all by encouraging detachment from desires and, consequently, promotes an experience of long-lasting peace.

Politics

The efforts to improve distribution of power among Khadi workers from different social positions require multiple mediations, within the Khadi sectors well as the larger social fabric. It demands a constant long-term engagement with the Khadi workforce, mainly through cultural interventions, as in the case of Charaka,[a] a women's multipurpose industrial cooperative society situated in Karnataka. The Charaka initiative is known not only for producing natural-dyed cotton handloom fabrics and garments but also for *Charaka Utsava*, an annual festival that provides a space for artisans to participate in cultural performances, seminars and discussions on social issues.

The cultural engagements help cultivate a sense of belonging among Khadi workers and encourage them to be part of a collective existence. There is also a similar need to promote intellectual pursuits like reading, writing and watching documentaries, while paying particular 'attention to the historical and social factors that shape societies and countries and to the diverse ways in which people organise their worlds' to deepen 'empathy' among the Khadi workforce.[12[p.302]] Meditation classes and programmes that encourage one to consider the perspective of others could be carried out to encourage compassion-building.[13,14] The visual and performing arts can become a medium for people to understand their nexus with the society and the environment. Art, being a creative medium, has the capacity to 'develop greater empathy for the circumstances of those with very different life experiences.'[15[p.37]] More importantly, Transactional Analysis programmes, that take a psychotherapeutic approach to understanding the interactions between individuals, could be organised by Khadi institutions to promote more effective communication and better management of interpersonal relationships within the community.[16,17]

To bring further positive changes within the larger social fabric in which the Khadi community is embedded, there is a need for a new education system, or *Nai Talim*, as envisaged by Gandhi which involves the 'all-round drawing out of the best in child and man—body, mind and spirit.'[18[p.197]] In essence, this new education is expected to enable individuals to govern themselves, inspire them to be their best and encourage them to lead others by example. The *Nai Talim* system of education recognises the 'knowledge found among the people.'[19[p.212]] It appreciates ordinary life and the work of farmers, artisans, small retailers and so on as knowledge-generating activities. It acknowledges the dialectical relationship present between material production and knowledge production. It emphasises on democratising knowledge and makes the development project inclusive for all.

The key features of *Nai Talim* education, as Kumarappa outlines, should employ human energy-based vocations as the medium of instruction around which all other intellectual subject matters should be taught.[20[p.188]] Further, education should be experiential and aided by art. It should kindle interest in phenomena, encouraging students to investigate why things are and what they are. It should advance from 'play to investigation and then to creation.'[20[p.189]] As much as possible, the *Nai talim* education centres should operate using funds generated through the sales of products produced from vocational training, relying on minimum external support. The Anand Niketan[b] school at *Sevagram ashram* in central India is inspired by the *Nai Talim* system of education. Here, children pursue intellectual learning in close integration with physical work, particularly undertaking activities such as gardening, cooking, spinning and so on.[21[p.6]] Such an exposure and space to help children see the dignity of physical labour could encourage them to take up occupations based on human energy, such as the Khadi activity, as prospective livelihoods.

Alternative media could also bring the life stories of those engaged in livelihoods based on physical labour into the public consciousness, thereby helping restore their lost self-respect. For instance, Project PARI (People's Archive of Rural India),[c] which documents life in rural India has provided an opportunity for village people to amplify their voices. A similar platform could be created exclusively for people from the Khadi sector to share their stories with the larger public and to establish a strong, tangible connection with the urban consumers.

The failure of Khadi occupations to be seen as aspirational livelihoods for people from across different social positions poses a threat to the survival of the sector in the long run, as discussed in the previous chapter. A possible way to overcome this challenge is to ensure that people earn a minimum living income. This issue is discussed in detail in the subsequent section on strengthening the economic self-sufficiency of the sector. Moreover, it is essential to dispense with the widespread belief held by the younger generation that physical work is drudgery. As Gandhi states, one should 'not discount the value of intellectual labour, but no amount of it is any compensation for bodily labour which every one of us is born to give for the common good of all.'[22[pp.355–6]] He continues,

It may be, often is, infinitely superior to bodily labour, but it never is or can be substitute for it, even as intellectual food though far superior to the grains we eat never can be a substitute for them. Indeed, without the products of the earth those of the intellect would be an impossibility.

There is a need to create interest in undertaking physical work by encouraging individuals to understand its moral and material implications. As Kumarappa remarks,

> [a] farmer, who has been educated to realise the social [and environmental] aspect[s] of his contribution and is enabled to see in every furrow he makes, the formation of life-giving channels which will carry food and hope to starving fellowmen, will take pleasure and pride in the role he plays in society and, obtaining satisfaction to his soul, will put his heart into his work. No tractor can do that. That is the only way to counteract drudgery. [23[p.19]]

The decentralisation of power dynamics requires a significant restructuring in the Khadi sector. There is a need for the state to accept the path of Swaraj Development Paradigm, and all of its plans should 'take a comprehensive view of the circumstances under which we are working—the needs of the people, the natural resources, facilities available to the meanest and, the quantity and quality of the human factor at our disposal.'[24[p.26]] According to S Rohini,

> [f]or preserving the ethos of Khadi, rather than just tinker with the existing system, a restructuring of the Khadi and Village Industries Commission is necessary. The potential of Khadi needs to be exploited for its inherent worth rather than be supported for charity. [25[p.12]]

The state should look to impose lower tax on the Khadi sector while levying more tax on machine-made textiles and its implements. As Kumarappa states,

> [w]here certain articles are produced both by centralised methods and by decentralised, as in the case of cloth or oil, price controls should be applied to mill products but not to hand-made goods, if we are to follow the fundamental principles of public finance and abstain from hampering the much desired distribution of wealth. [26[p.60]]

Such price control encourages the consumption of more environment-friendly and socially-just textiles. The state has to provide basic living wages and incentives based on performance to sustain the motivation of the people employed. Importantly, the employees of the state being public servants should be paid in line with the average earnings of ordinary citizens. According to Kumarappa, '[a]nything much above that will be diverging too far from the condition of the people we [state] profess to serve.'[20[p.117]] This would encourage such employees to understand the problems confronted by ordinary workers. It is essential that recruitment of individuals for state-level operations are made based on necessary qualifications, including first-hand experience in Khadi production and marketing. Such a policy would reduce the disconnect between bureaucrats and Khadi producers.

In addition, the state should gradually withdraw from direct Khadi production and sales activities over a period of five years. A similar recommendation was also made by a recent evaluation study, which stated, '[l]ike in any other sector, the government agency should not get into the business of doing business... The product development and marketing of Khadi products should be left to the private sector.'[27[p.14]] Instead, the state should restrict its activities and operate as an oversight agency to protect the authenticity of Khadi. Removing itself from directly running Khadi activities and its associated financial management would help to reduce the corruption and red-tape that are rife within the state machinery by minimising the financial transactions that it intermediates. Further, as Kumarappa points out, 'arrangements must be made [by the state] that no one, however highly placed, is immune from enquiry if allegations against him are made by responsible parties and a prima facie case exists.'[24[p.22]] This would help restore the public's confidence in bureaucracy. More importantly, to tackle corruption within the state machinery, people should be encouraged to select representatives of high moral standards, 'capable of [a] disinterested approach to problems and of deciding matters on merit even against themselves.'[24[p.22]]

The monitoring could entail frequent inspections of production and sales entities to ensure the authenticity of Khadi rather than controlling the sector through trademark. The definition of authenticity should be guided by a holistic definition of Khadi textiles based on the conception of swaraj that includes fabrics produced from hand spinning, hand weaving and other hand-crafted value additions using native varieties of cotton. As suggested by scholars D Dhanuraj and others, 'any deviation from the defined processes to improve productivity is welcome, but should be marked out as a different product with a different brand.'[27[p.16]] The district level authorities of the state could act as audit agencies to prevent spurious Khadi production and marketing within their territories by imposing legal sanctions.

Further, the monitoring agency would need to ensure that maximum limits over the scale of production are set for each Khadi institution, replacing the current minimum thresholds. Such caps on production would encourage more people to take up the activity by curbing monopolies within the sector. The monitoring process should require Khadi institutions to follow a coding system that indicates the specificity of products, like yarn spun on '*takli*,' or '*ambar Charkha*,' woven on 'frame loom' or 'pit loom,' dyed using 'natural dyes' or 'azo free dyes' or 'chemical dyes,' printed using 'hand blocks' or 'screen print' and so on. It would help Khadi institutions to fix different prices for products produced via different processes while informing and educating consumers about the products' history and enabling them to pay accordingly.[27[p.15]]

This shift in the role of the state would create a ground for Khadi institutions to self-rule. The lack of participatory space within the existing institutional framework of Khadi institutions can be rectified by ensuring that decision-making processes rely on consensus rather than majority rule. For such a process to be effective, the size of the institution needs to be maintained at an optimum scale. It is crucial to make sure that the scale of a Khadi institution is within the optimum size of 50 people, which Kirkpatrick Sale suggests as the highest possible number to effectively reach an agreement at the workplace.[28[p.247]] Hemanth, a social entrepreneur who has a long-standing association with the Khadi sector, says, 'We should have more institutions with fewer people instead of the other way round.' The scale of the Khadi activity has to be reoriented towards greater horizontal expansion rather than vertical growth. There is a need to make sure that when any necessary aid is accepted, it does not wrest decision making power from the Khadi institutions. The end goal should be to help protect and preserve the self-rule of the Khadi workers.

Further, the state has allowed manufacture, import, and use of machine made and polyester national flags from the year 2022 by amending the Flag Code of India. Whereas, the provisions of The Emblems and Names (Prevention of improper use) Act, 1950 and the successive Flag Code of India, 2002 had ensured Khadi as the only textile that can be used in the manufacture and use of national flag. It was a conscious decision taken in the newly formed Constituent Assembly in the year 1947 and stood as a testimony for the commitment as a nation to the spirit of swaraj and in turn for a non-violent social order.

With this new amendment, the government intends to promote mass production and extensive use of national flags as a part of celebrating 75th year of independence. The state wants to encourage 'citizens to pledge to re-dedicate themselves to the tricolour for the development, bright future, and security of the country by hoisting Tricolour in their homes.'[29] However, the national flag without Khadi clearly shows the disharmony between word and deed, thereby making the government sponsored nationalism a hypocrisy. Therefore, it is necessary for the state to withdraw the amendment and reinstate Khadi produced in the country as the sole textile for manufacturing and the use of national flag.

There is a need for a network of Khadi institutions in Karnataka to act as a collective force to resist the coercive pressures of the state and non-state actors. A similar recommendation has also been made by P Gopinath, who suggests that it would help to 'improve the low standard of living of the working poor through collective, purposeful manipulation of the public environment—public action—whether by means of legislation, lobbying or self-organisation.'[30[p.332]] The network should strengthen solidarity among Khadi institutions by offering voluntary membership and ensuring that they are autonomous and legally independent entities, as in the case of the Mondragón corporation in Spain.[31[pp.279,283]]

The Mondragón corporation, started in the 1940s, was established by a young social Catholic priest, José Maria Arizmendiarrieta, with the intention of providing better education and employment to youths just after the Spanish Civil War. He combined the entrepreneurial spirit of Spain's industrial tradition and the communitarian values of the rural hinterland to create a series of cooperatives.[32] He initially established *Escuela Profesional*, a technical training school, in 1943 that led to the Talleres Ulgor, the first cooperative that fabricated heater and gas stoves. Over the years, new cooperatives were added to form the Mondragón corporation, which currently comprises over 260 firms employing more than 80,000 workers.

Collective action through a network of Khadi institutions is essential to protect the interest of the sector, and could emulate an organisation like the SEWA (Self Employed Women's Association), the largest trade union in India. The SEWA was established in 1972 as a response to the unfair and corrupt practices of cloth merchants that had kept the earnings of women labourers low, pushing them into a precarious position. The idea of organising women labourers under the umbrella of SEWA was conceived by Ela Bhatt, a lawyer deeply influenced by Mahatma Gandhi's thought. With its success as a union, various cooperatives were formed over the years to help its members produce and market the fruits of their labour and build their assets. Since then, it has managed to improve the lives of poor women from across different informal sectors, 'through both, the collective pressure that organising allows them to exert and the creation of alternative employment opportunities.'[33[p.1]] At present, it consists of over 100 cooperatives with more than 13,000,000 members across the country.

The proposed Khadi network should make decisions based on consensus, provide basic living wages and incentives based on performance to ensure efficiency at work and set a fixed ratio between the highest paid and lowest paid to curb income inequality within the institutional structure of the network. The network has to develop systems for ensuring the financial and social security of Khadi workers. It should also launch district Khadi promotion centres to facilitate networking between Khadi institutions and wholesale buyers. Regular consumer awareness drives could be carried out to bring Khadi into the fold of public consciousness. Further, they could facilitate training programmes for Khadi workers as well as aspirants who want to join the sector. The entrepreneur programmes could equip participants with skills required for better management of production and marketing of Khadi products, similar to the Handloom School[d] initiative of the WomenWeave charitable trust in Madhya Pradesh. The school provides training to young handloom weavers from across India in skills that help them to optimise marketing opportunities and to earn more sustainable livelihoods.

The network should also provide training programmes for Khadi workers to undertake non-violent resistance in the form of *satyagraha*. Such an effort is essential to establish and maintain non-violent social order within the Khadi sector. This kind of training should aim at helping individuals realise how their passiveness towards oppression contributes to the propagation of existing oppressive conditions. Individuals should be trained to practice *satyagraha* in their everyday life. As philosopher R B Gregg outlines, such a training could include reading and discussions about non-violent struggles within the optimum group size of 5–12.[34[pp.149–75]] Non-violent tactics need to be explored in various scenarios, with clear reasons provided for opting specific strategies. Further, Gregg advises the practice of speaking in a low, calm, gentle and evenly pitched tone of voice. Importantly, patience, self-control and courtesy in everyday functions of life have to be exercised, too. Self-less actions can be carried out and results can be acknowledged. Self-respect must be developed with humility and tempered by humour to check notions of superiority. Storytelling and watching films of heroic achievements can be done to enhance courage.

Belief in unity with fellow humans can be strengthened through group activities such as meditation, singing, dancing, walks, cooking, undertaking manual work and serving people in need. However, as Gandhi points out, it is important to make the trainees understand the necessary conditions for the success of *satyagraha*:

'(1) The *Satyagrahi* [the person who undertakes *satyagraha*] should not have any hatred in his heart against the opponent; (2) the issue must be true and substantial; (3) The *Satyagrahi* must be prepared to suffer till the end for his cause.'[35[p.64]]

There is a need to establish a centre for Khadi research and technology under the network of Khadi institutions. The centre should function according to 'non-violent science' rooted in the Swaraj Development Paradigm.[36[p.3721]] According to Kumarappa:

Science is not the creation of man. Nature works in well-defined grooves according to immutable laws. When man understands these laws and reduces them to a system of knowledge, we call it science. It follows, therefore, that any course of action to be termed scientific should conform to nature in all its bearings and where we deviate from nature, to that extent we are unscientific.[37[p.1]]

The key features of such a science can be drawn from management scholar Shambu Prasad's pioneering work on experiments made during the Khadi movement in the early 20th century.[38[p.199],39] According to Prasad, the central objective of non-violent science is to attain swaraj though experimentation, both in institutional and technical spheres. Non-violent science acknowledges the incapacity of humans to understand absolute Truth in its entirety. The universality of non-violent science lies in a sense that every individual can be a scientist without the requirement of costly research equipment. By encouraging people's participation in the making of technology, it provides space for end users to be involved at the design stage itself. This, in turn, avoids the necessity for end users to adopt readymade technologies.

Furthermore, by keeping the production and diffusion of knowledge intact, it eliminates the development of hierarchies of knowledge between the scientists as experts and others as mere end users. This was observed in the call for the participation of 'farmers and enthusiasts to build a knowledge base of the varieties of Indian cotton through large scale experimentation across the country at various farms and regions' by the All India Spinners Association (AISA) in 1949, during the

Khadi movement.[38[p.19]] As a part of the exercise, AISA set the research parameters and interested farmers were provided with information on the techniques of pure line selection of cotton varieties and on the durability and maturity of fibres over staple length. The farmers carried out experimentation on their farms and shared their findings with AISA. With the farmers recast as both scientists as well as beneficiaries, the project reduced the hierarchies of knowledge.

The non-violent science aims at producing a new plural knowledge system using vernacular knowledge and proven practices of prevailing science.[39] In doing so, it bypasses the binary opposition of tradition and modernity. It requires scientists to not only conduct experimentation based on reasons and facts but also with the intention of abetting a morality of non-violence that fosters the greatest good of all. It calls for a new regulation of intellectual property rights that treats scientists as trustees of their knowledge and considers innovations as open source. By recognising the limited control that individuals have over the ultimate outcomes of their actions, non-violent science considers failure as an opportunity for exploring uncharted territories that others can learn from and a significant contribution to the existing knowledge base. It comprehends research as a vital social process, promotes methodological diversity and sees the possibility of continual improvement through experimentation.

Non-violent science emphasises a close connection between research labs and the field. It encourages labs to be self-supporting, as Kumarappa puts it, '[a]n agricultural college, which cannot maintain itself on the land allotted to it, belies the object for which it exists. Similarly, all other professional and technical colleges should be made to pay for themselves.'[20[p.192]] This helps scientists to develop sensitivity to every crisis that people experience on ground when their innovations and recommendations are adopted. It urges labs to seek validation for their inventions from people on the field. Non-violent science advocates a field-to-lab-to-field approach, contrary to the prevailing unidirectional lab-to-field approach of mainstream scientific research. It also prioritises the quality of the output, understood in terms of social and environmental impact, over the productivity of a technology.

By emphasising 'a science by the people,' a Khadi science and technology centre has to depart from the model prevalent in current scientific establishments that is rooted in the assumption of science—created by scientists—for the people. Useful pointers can be found in the contemporary 'humanitarian design' approach that involves collaborative processes between designers and beneficiaries that 'account for power and knowledge dynamics, and that at their best embrace indigenous and collective ways of knowing and living.'[40[p.43]] Insights into the non-violent scientific approach of field-to-lab-to-field can be obtained from the Honeybee Network[e] initiative in India, which 'pools and links both formal and informal science and scientists.'[41] Apart from conducting research on Khadi technologies, the centre for Khadi research and technology has to initiate programmes to inculcate an attitude of research and experimentation among the Khadi community and to employ vernacular languages in scientific journals, books and conferences.

A much-needed technological intervention at the moment is the development of small-scale, low-cost cotton processing machines from ginning to rovings. This would help Khadi institutions to run and operate their own cotton processing units. As Kalleshi, a pioneer of Khadi revival in Karnataka, states, 'There has to be decentralisation in producing rovings. Khadi institutions should be able to buy their cotton directly from farmers.' Such an intervention, in turn, would considerably enhance the freedom of Khadi institutions. Decentralised cotton processing units enable cotton farmers and Khadi institutions to directly interact with one another, thus benefitting them. A case in point is the Malkha[f] initiative in Telangana, which aimed to develop an alternative to the industrial model of cotton processing. The Malkha model of producing handloom cotton fabrics has allowed the group to source locally-grown cotton from marginal farmers and to ensure the diversity of cotton varieties. This has enabled them to manufacture cotton fabrics with unique textures and to diversify the cotton fabrics in the market. Additionally, the decentralised cotton processing machines could

> spur a shift in cotton cultivation towards more sustainable patterns, renewing interest in traditional and perennial varieties of cotton that suffer from lack of local markets that can convert cotton to yarn. The recent organic cotton movement is also likely to benefit from such technological innovation. [36[pp.246–7]]

It is important for the network of Khadi institutions to become resilient and adaptive to the ever-evolving circumstances that affect the sector. They can take insights from Gram Seva Sangh[g] (GSS), an organisation that works to protect and nurture the handmade sector in the state of Karnataka. The work of GSS involves organising long marches, cultural events, symposiums and, more recently, pressuring for tax exemptions on the handmade sector through *satyagraha*, specifically with hunger strikes. Carrying out such protests would help to bring back Khadi into the fold of public consciousness and ensure its survival in the long run. Similarly, the network needs to work with the government and ensure the policies are conducive for the Khadi sector to thrive. Further, efforts should be made to strengthen democratic process within the state machinery. Pointers can be taken from the work of Mazdoor Kisan Shakti Sangathan[h] (MKSS), a people's organisation that works with peasants and labourers of Rajasthan to strengthen participatory democracy. It has played a pioneering role in getting the important Right to Information (RTI) act that mandates timely response to citizen requests for government information by the public authorities.

The disorganisation within Khadi institutions due to the neglectful attitude of managers can be resolved through inducing them to be more efficient in their work by connecting their income to production or sales of Khadi products. Similarly, the cooperation among workers can be enhanced by setting up group targets to create mutual obligations among them. The Khadi institutions should consider only workers as primary members, and encourage them to become investors. Ensuring financial stake and liability to everyone who is part of the institution can foster a sense of ownership and voluntary responsibility. There is also a need for a fair income and profit-distribution mechanism within the Khadi institutions.

Economy

The regimented working conditions at the CSP could be scrapped if Khadi institutions set up their own small cotton processing units. It is important to note that cotton processing, up until the stage of rovings, can only be done by machines because hand processing is economically unviable. However, such a power-operated small-scale cotton processing does not provide the wholesome work envisioned by the development paradigm as it involves monotonous work without much scope for creativity. Therefore, it is essential to set up rotations in the occupation or make it part-time for workers in order to break the tedious routine. For the same reason, the spinning process, too, should be considered as a part-time occupation, and not full time, owing to a lack of creative space in using the new model of spinning machines. Efforts to mechanise spinning and weaving should be shunned because it effectively eliminates the uniqueness of Khadi, which lies in the handspun and handwoven production.

There is a need for Khadi institutions to encourage their workers to establish self-help groups (SHGs)[i] to improve their financial situation. This could assist them to save money regularly and provide an easier access to much-needed credit. The increasing negative perception of work in the Khadi sector can be reversed by assuring a minimum living wage[j] of Rs 400 ($5) per day, as is aspired to by a large section of Khadi workers. Even though challenging to implement, such an effort demands the effective marketing of Khadi products at higher prices. Therefore, it becomes essential to tap into emerging markets, high-end exhibitions and e-commerce platforms. An example of such an initiative is Metaphor Racha,[k] a boutique based in Bengaluru. The boutique sources Khadi materials for a fair price from various Khadi institutions in Karnataka and transforms them into attractive garments. It has successfully managed to market them for the last ten years, mainly through exhibitions and e-commerce platforms. Similar ventures adopting 'new marketing techniques' have to be initiated by Khadi institutions to survive in the contemporary marketplace.[43[p.390]]

Khadi institutions should involve individuals who have the necessary marketing skills or train their salespeople to use such avenues. Importantly, they should produce diverse Khadi products and explore collaborations with other boutiques or alternative sales entities. This would eliminate 'the benefits availed of by the intermediaries.'[27[p.15]] According to Ravi, a designer who works closely with a Khadi institution,

> At the moment, the revival of the handmade sector is difficult through cooperatives. I think individuals who are interested in crafts should go to villages and work with one or two artisans. I strongly believe that if we offer continuous work and fair wages, many people will prefer to stay back in their villages and continue their craft.

Small efforts, such as sustaining one or two artisans, can act as a starting point for rebuilding a deteriorating handmade sector like Khadi. However, it requires a more flexible institutional framework that permits Khadi institutions to enter into smaller collaborations. The state has the potential to stimulate demand for Khadi products and sustain Khadi institutions. It needs to prioritise Khadi textile consumption and encourage Khadi outfits among its employees. Instead of placing a single large order as in the case of the army, it should recommend the state wings to purchase as much as possible from their own regional Khadi institutions, while ensuring a diversity of Khadi textiles. As Kumarappa advises, such purchases of products produced by the masses act as a way for the state to return the 'power and finance' derived from the public.[24[p.136]] However, Khadi institutions have to 'step-up the publicity of the Khadi products in order for them to enter the mainstream market.'[44[p.101]]

There is a place for different organisations and entities to act as an interface between Khadi institutions and the market. For example, Dastakar Andhra,[l] a public charitable trust in Andhra Pradesh, has established a long-term association with four handloom weaving cooperatives, and supports them in production, warehousing and marketing. Khamir,[m] a handicraft promotional trust in Gujarat, has made commitments to support artisans by offering six months of assured purchase of its products, along with providing advances, raw materials and design inputs. Similar arrangements would help Khadi institutions to sell their products and assure a gainful employment for its workers.

Another potential way of marketing Khadi products would be through a network of retail stores, similar to what is seen with the Organic Farmers' Market (OFM)[n] in Chennai. The case of OFM is examined in detail, as it provides a number of potential insights for the Khadi sector. The OFM was started by a few friends with the intention of supporting farmers through fair prices and to bring back the lost self-respect among the farming community. Initially, in 2008, they established a volunteer-driven organic store called Restore. With the success of its unique marketing strategy of placing farmers at the centre of business, new stores were added over the years to form OFM, a network of 15 independent organic retail stores with one common collection point that procures produce from organic farmers.

The OFM is not a registered body but decisions are taken collectively by the entrepreneurs of all its retail outlets. The different outlets under the umbrella of OFM are connected through a collectively agreed list of norms.[45] The list compels the outlets to not make large investments in the set-up and running of the outlet, so that it can be affordably replicated by others. It demands a notice board in every outlet with the details of the sourcing of each product to enable consumers to cross-check the authenticity of organic products and the cost of production. More importantly, it recommends flat slab rates to provide consumers the same price on vegetables throughout the year and to ensure predictable prices for farmers. The list of norms advises entrepreneurs at every outlet to make monthly farm visits to ensure the authenticity of organic produce and prevent the sale of products produced by organisations other than women's groups and farmers' collectives. It obligates entrepreneurs of the outlets to source all products only from the main collection points and to direct customers to their nearest outlet. It allows the addition of a maximum of 20% margin over the procurement price and requires outlet entrepreneurs to make payments to farmers within a week of the delivery of products. Lastly, it urges OFM to offer no credits to its entrepreneurs and advises outlets to organise awareness programmes and events on organic food and organic farming.

This unique marketing strategy, based on the norms outlined above, has helped created a regular customer base driven by trust. The consumers provide financial and other necessary forms of assistance to the OFM when there is a need. About 200 farmers are supported by the OFM. They are encouraged to come and sell their products directly to consumers in events frequently organised under the banner 'Meet Your Farmers.' The successful model of OFM could be adopted by existing Khadi institutions to strengthen the conscious exchange between producers and consumers.

The widening chasm between the production and consumption of Khadi has become a barrier for the expansion of moral consciousness. Efforts to create consumer awareness among local communities are essential to break this barrier. The moral and material implications of buying locally-produced goods have to be explained to the consumers through various communication channels. Long-term engagement with local communities helps to encourage the local consumption of Khadi products and provides fair opportunities for both producers and consumers in their exchange.

Similarly, self-consumption of Khadi products among the producers has to be encouraged to realise the spirit of self-sufficiency. As Kumarappa says, producers 'should take the first step necessary to revive [their] industry by placing a higher value on [their] own handicraft, and not patronise foreign articles in preference.'[20[p.83]] However, it is essential to make sure that Khadi workers earn a minimum living income so that they can afford their own products. Furthermore, respect for their products has to be increased by explaining the moral and material implications of economic self-sufficiency. This could encourage them to consume their own Khadi products.

Consumer awareness about the implication of buying Khadi products on society, and the environment at large, has to be created in urban centres. As Ravi, a Khadi advocate, points out, 'Khadi should become aspirational. We need to communicate. That is where we have failed.' Consumers can take the responsibility of arresting the spread of fake Khadi by purchasing only authentic Khadi. Kumarappa writes thus on this subject:

> If the goods come from a source which may be tainted with exploitation, either of sweat labour or of the political, financial or economic hold over other nations, or classes, or races, then the

buyer of such goods, will be a party to such exploitation, just as a person who buys stolen articles from a *chore bazar* creates a market for stolen goods and thus will be encouraging the art of stealing. Therefore, anyone who buys goods indiscriminately is not discharging her full responsibility when the sole criterion of her buying is merely the low price or the good quality of the goods. Hence, we should buy goods only from sources from which full information is readily available and which source can be brought under our influence; otherwise, we shall have to shoulder a share of the blame for sweated labour, political slavery, or economic stranglehold. We cannot absolve ourselves of all blame by merely pleading ignorance in regard to the source.[20[p.78]]

As elucidated above, consumers need to be better informed about product history, including the production processes utilised and the working conditions of the producers. Such consumer activism requires them to buy products produced close to their places of residence, so that they have the opportunity to make visits to the production centres and to see first-hand how the textiles are manufactured. There is a need to create a space for direct interaction between producers and consumers, so that they can better understand each other. For example, Ragi Kana,° a weekly market in Bengaluru, provides an opportunity for urban consumers to interact and purchase handmade products directly from rural producers. It facilitates talks, discussions, film screenings and cultural events to bridge the ever-increasing disconnect between the producer and the consumer. Khadi institutions can also organise regular field visits for urban consumers to help them understand the manufacture of Khadi products. This can help establish a stronger bond between both the parties and, in turn, help strengthen the Khadi supply chain. Such interactions with the producers and familiarity with the production process enhance empathy among consumers and help them understand the cost of production. It motivates purchasers to pay more for Khadi products and to distinguish Khadi from other, less expensive handloom and power loom textiles. Direct interactions can also boost the self-respect of the workers and in turn helps to make Khadi a more aspirational occupation.

Finally, it is essential to create consumer awareness about the care and disposal of Khadi garments. To ensure a longer lifespan of the products, Khadi institutions need to instruct them about the need to handwash and dry them in the shade to avoid damaging the fabric. Khadi institutions can create an avenue for returning used Khadi materials for upcycling. The implications of disposal on the environment and society have to be explained to consumers through different communication channels. This would foster the creation of more aware and responsible consumers.

Notes

a More about Charaka can be found at http://charaka.in.
b More about the Anand Niketan school can be found at http://www.anandaniketan.info.
c More about the People's Archive or Rural India (PARI) can be found at https://ruralindiaonline.org.
d More about the Handloom School can be found at https://www.womenweave.org/The%20Handloom%20School.
e More information about Honeybee Network can be found at http://honeybee.org.
f More information about Malkha can be found at https://malkha.in.
g More about Gram Seva Sangh can be found at https://gramsevasangh.org.
h More about Mazdoor Kisan Shakti Sangathan can be found at http://mkssindia.org.
i Self-help groups are financially intermediary committees usually composed of 10–20 members voluntarily coming together from similar socio-economic backgrounds to save small sums of money on a regular basis.
j The living wage aspired to by the Khadi community is closer to Rs 375 (£4) per day, a sum recommended by an internal committee of the Labour Ministry, Government of India. The recommended figure is calculated for a person having a partner and two children below the age of 14.[42]
k More about Metaphor Racha can be found at https://www.metaphorracha.com.
l More about Dastakar Andhra can be found at http://www.dastkarandhra.org.
m More about Khamir can be found at https://www.khamir.org.
n More about Organic Farmers' Market (OFM) can be found at http://www.ofmtn.in.
o More about Ragi Kana can be found at https://ragikana.wordpress.com and https://www.facebook.com/ragikana/.

References

1 Nagaraj DR. In: Shobhi PDC, editor. *The flaming feet and other essays: The Dalit movement in India.* Ranikhet: Permanent black; 2010.
2 Dharampal. *Bharatiya Chitta, Manas and Kala. Essays on tradition, recovery and freedom.* Mapusa: Other India Press; 2007.
3 Terchek R. *Gandhi: Struggling for autonomy.* Lanham, MD: Rowman & Littlefield; 1998.
4 James GA. *Ecology is permanent economy: The activism and environmental philosophy of Sunderlal Bahuguna.* Albany: State University of New York Press; 2013.

5 Prasanna. Why we need to remember the civilised Rama, and not the angry one. *The Indian Express* [Internet]. 2019 Oct 28 [cited 2020 Mar 19]; Available from: https://indianexpress.com/article/express-sunday-eye/dont-look-back-in-anger-ramayana-ayodhya-mahatma-gandhi-kaidasa-6085475/

6 Gowda C. The Ramayana as a plea for Grama Rajya. *Deccan Herald* [Internet]. Bangalore; 2019 Sep 1 [cited 2020 Mar 19]; Available from: https://www.deccanherald.com/opinion/the-ramayana-as-a-plea-for-grama-rajya-758404.html

7 Feral C. The connectedness model and optimal development: Is ecopsychology the answer to emotional well-being? *The Humanistic Psychologist.* 1998;26(1–3):243–73.

8 Metz M. *Back to nature: The impact of nature relatedness on empathy and narcissism in the millennial generation.* Virginia: James Madison University; 2014.

9 Piff PK, Dietze P, Feinberg M, Stancato DM, Keltner D. Awe, the small self, and prosocial behaviour. *Journal of Personality and Social Psychology.* 2015;108(6):883–99.

10 Richardson M, Cormack A, McRobert L, Underhill R. 30 days wild: Development and evaluation of a large-scale nature engagement campaign to improve well-being. *PLoS ONE.* 2016;11(2):e0149777.

11 Williams F. *The nature fix—Why nature makes us happier, healthier, and more creative.* New York: W. W. Norton & Company; 2017.

12 Schwittay A, Boocock K. Experiential and empathetic engagements with global poverty: 'Live below the line so that others can rise above it'. *Third World Quarterly.* 2015;36(2):291–305.

13 Condon P, Desbordes G, Miller WB, DeSteno D. Meditation increases compassionate responses to suffering. *Psychological Science.* 2013;24(10):2125–7.

14 Weisz E, Zaki J. Empathy-building interventions: A review of existing work and suggestions for future directions. In: Seppälä EM, Simon-Thomas E, Brown SL, Worline MC, Cameron CD, Doty JR, editors. *The Oxford handbook of compassion science* (pp. 205–18). Oxford: Oxford University Press; 2017.

15 MacNeill K, Coles A, Kokkinos A, Robertson M. *Promoting gender equality through the arts and creative industries: A review of case studies and evidence.* Melbourne: Victorian Health Promotion Foundation; 2018.

16 Berne E. *Transactional analysis in psychotherapy.* New York: Grove Press; 1961.

17 Davidson C, Mountain A. *Working together: Organizational transactional analysis and business performance.* Farnham: Gower Publishing Limited; 2011.

18 Gandhi MK. Education. *Harijan.* 1937 July 31.

19 Basole A. Gandhian economics in a knowledge society. In: Sethia T, Narayan A, editors. *The living Gandhi: Lessons for our times* (pp. 211–77). New Delhi: Penguin Books India; 2013.

20 Kumarappa JC. *Why the village movement?* Wardha, India: All India Village Industries Association; 1936.

21 Anand Niketan School, Nai Talim Samiti. Anand Niketan: Annual Report 2015–2016. Sewagram; 2016.

22 Gandhi MK. Necessity of bodily labour. *Young India.* 1925 Oct 15.

23 Kumarappa JC. *The Gandhian economy and other essays.* Wardha: All India Village Industries Association; 1949.

24 Kumarappa JC. *Planning by the people for the people.* Ahmedabad: Navajivan Press; 1954.

25 Rohini S. Whither khadi? *Economic and Political Weekly.* 2009;44(13):12–15.

26 Kumarappa JC. *Swaraj for the masses.* Wardha: Akhil Bharat Serva Seva Sangh; 1948.

27 Dhanuraj D, Nair L, Varghese JP. *How to revive the Khadi sector—An evaluation with special focus on Khadi act.* Kochi: Centre for Public Policy Research; 2018.

28 Sale K. *Human scale revisited: A new look at the classic case for a decentralist future.* Vermont: Chelsea Green Publishing; 2017.

29 Business Standard News. Explained: The Flag Code of India, the amendments and the objections [Internet]. 2022 [cited 2022 Jul 31]. Available from: https://www.business-standard.com/article/current-affairs/explained-the-flag-code-of-india-the-amendments-and-the-objections-122072501327_1.html

30 Gopinath P. Wages, working conditions and socio-economic mobility of spinners and weavers in the unorganised Khadi industry: Findings from a survey in India. *The Indian Journal of Labour Economics.* 2010;53(2):305–38.

31 Barandiaran X, Lezaun J. The Mondragón experience. In: Michie J, Blasi JR, Borzaga C, editors. *The Oxford handbook of mutual, co-operative, and co-owned business* (pp. 279–94). Oxford: Oxford University Press; 2017.

32 Molina F, Miguez A. The origins of Mondragon: Catholic co-operativism and social movement in a Basque Valley (1941–59). *Social History.* 2008;33(3):284–98.

33 Blaxall J. *India's Self-Employed Women's Association (SEWA)—Empowerment through mobilization of poor women on a large scale.* Washingto DC: World Bank; 2004.

34 Gregg RB. *The power of nonviolence.* New York: Schocken Books; 1966.

35 Gandhi MK. The non-violent sanction. *Harijan.* 1946 Mar 31.

36 Prasad S. Towards an understanding of Gandhi's views on science. *Economic and Political Weekly.* 2001;36(39):3721–32.

37 Kumarappa JC. *Science and progress.* Wardha: All India Village Industries Association; 1948.

38 Prasad CS. Suicide deaths and quality of Indian cotton: Perspectives from history of technology and khadi movement. *Economic and Political Weekly.* 1999;34(5):12–21.

39 Prasad CS. Prayog in design education: Lessons from the khadi archive. In: Katiyar VS, Mehta S, editors. *Design education: Tradition and modernity (Scholastic Papers from the International Conference, DETM 05).* Ahmedabad: National Institute of Design; 2007.

40 Schwittay A. Designing development: Humanitarian design in the financial inclusion assemblage. *Political and Legal Anthropology Review.* 2014;37(1):29–47.

41 Gupta AK. The Honeybee Network: Voices from grassroots innovators. *Cultural Survival Quarterly Magazine.* 1996;58(1):57–60.

42 Nanda PK. ₹375 minimum wage plan junked as govt opts for ₹2 hike. *Livemint* [Internet]. 2019 [cited 2020 May 7]. Available from: https://www.livemint.com/news/india/rs-375-minimum-wage-plan-junked-as-govt-opts-for-rs-2-hike-1563035733771.html

43 Ahmad R. Journey of Khadi and Village Industries: 'livery of freedom' to 'fabric of livelihood'. *Scholarly Research Journal for Interdisciplinary Studies.* 2013;2(8):382–92.
44 Goel N, Jain K. Revival of Khadi—An analysis of the state of khadi in India with supply and demand side problems. *Innovative Journal of Business and Management.* 2015;4(5):100–3.
45 Kuruganti K. Retailing, with a world of difference: Empowering farmers & consumers the 'organic farmers' (OFM) market' way. *Vikalp Sangam* [Internet]. 2017. Available from: http://www.vikalpsangam. org/static/media/uploads/Vikalp%20Sangam%20Case%20Studies/ retailingofmkavithakuruganti.pdf

6 Janapada Khadi

An Exemplary of Swaraj Development Paradigm

The growing disconnection between theory and practice all around the world has pushed former into mere intellectual pursuit without any reference to the very material concerns of everyday living and latter into a life of monotony and stagnation. I believe that a true theoretical insight arises out of everyday observation and problem solving over a long-term engagement with ordinary people. Similarly, I also feel that, a theoretical insight fulfils its purpose only when deployed to address the fundamental concern of the ordinary people. This theory-practice dialogue fundamentally makes thoughts and actions of Gandhi and Kumarappa resonate even after so many decades of their demise. As a part of continuing this theory-praxis tradition, in this chapter, I would like to show the feasibility of many pragmatic steps that have been suggested in the previous chapter through my own efforts of aligning Janapada Khadi[a] activity of Janapada Seva Trust[b] in line with the swaraj development paradigm. Janapada Seva Trust is a voluntary organisation based at Melukote, a small town situated in southern Karnataka. It was started by my grandparents Surendra Koulagi and Girija Koulagi in the year 1960 inspired by the thoughts of Mahatma Gandhi. Janapada Khadi being one of the important activities of the Trust since 1980s, it was run like any other Khadi activity in the country with the narrow intention of providing livelihood security for rural poor. However, the key difference between Janapada Khadi and other Khadi institutions was in its decision to sustain the activity entirely based on the support of the masses without any financial aid from the state.

I decided to join Janapda Khadi initiative right after the completion of my doctorate in early 2020. This chapter depicts my own journey of translating swaraj development theory into practice. As an initial step, I started to redefine the objective of Janapada Khadi from Khadi production to establishing swaraj or a non-violent community where individuals can have more control over their lives without exploiting

DOI: 10.4324/9781003353096-9

one another. Several efforts have been made over the last two years to achieve the objective in all the three interconnected spheres of morality, politics and economy.

Morality

As a part of community development programmes, many activities such as prayers, theatre, documentary screenings, transactional analysis classes, potlucks, exposure visits, book reading and many other events are held once in a month to encourage members of Janapada Khadi to recognise the Truth of interconnectedness of life and in turn realise good of an individual is embedded in the good of all. The impact of these various exercises on the morals of people is quite visible. Savitha, a senior weaver, comments on the prayer meeting that takes place every day at the workplace. 'It is like a daily reminder for us that we are all one,' she says. The prayers include elements of all faiths and used to be sung at *ashrams* set up by Gandhi. By taking the names of Gods that are worshipped in different religions and by creatively weaving them as various manifestations of the same God, the prayers provide a basis for reinterpreting cultural memory. The subtle acceptance of oneness, as expressed in Savitha's statement, shows the capacity of cultural memories to be recast and for worldviews to be widened. Such an exegetical engagement can help reshape the cultural memories of Khadi workers and align them with the Swaraj Development Paradigm.

Similarly, environmental education has significantly helped to encourage people to recognise the relationship between self and the other. For example, Pallavi, a weaver states that 'I enjoy bird watching. I am amazed to see the intricate relationship that exists in nature, which we are a part of.' These community development activities have also enhanced the sense of belongingness. Geetha, a warper, notes, 'I like working here because along with the work, we are encouraged to participate in dramas, singing, group games and so on. We are all like a family here.' Similarly, art has significantly enhanced empathy among the workers. For example, Prakash, a dyer says,

> Last year, we performed a skit focused on gender discrimination. I played a role of woman. The exercise helped me realise how we [men] dominate women every day. Since then, I have been trying, at least, to listen patiently to the points that my wife makes.

Even though enormous efforts are made to recognise the Truth of interconnectedness of life, the different social positions shaped by gender, caste, education and age are still a barrier. For example, Savitha, a weaver, explains:

> Even though we speak about the fallacy of the caste system in our regular prayer meetings, many of the upper-caste people still practice discrimination based on caste at the workplace. Discrimination occurs not only with respect to work, but also in other occasions such as during potlucks. They do not eat what I bring from my home since I am a *Dalit*. I feel terrible that this is happening even here.

However, enterprise being a small group of a dozen people without a hierarchy provides space to resolve differences. It is evident that, working with the morals of people is a continuous process. Further, Transactional Analysis, a psychotherapeutic approach has equipped people to better manage their interpersonal relationships. For example, Pallavi, a weaver, states that 'Transactional analysis programmes have taught me how to interact with people without much friction. It has helped to have better relationships with others at workplace as well as in my family.' In short, tractional analysis has significantly helped to improve human relations within the enterprise.

Politics

The first challenge in terms of power relations was to dismantle the hierarchical relationship of owner and wage labourer existed between the governing body of Janapada Seva Trust and Khadi workers. A major institutional innovation was proposed to dismantle this hierarchy. However, the need of a leadership was recognised and a role of coordinator who coordinates the various aspects of the enterprise was created. An institutional framework was evolved where ownership is equally shared among workers, the coordinator and the Janapada Seva Trust. By doing so, it was aimed to establish a system where everyone who is part of the enterprise becomes an owner as well as a worker.

I decided to take up that role of coordinator and started to discuss this new three stake holder model with others. Initially there was a clear resistance from the workers' end because the proposed ownership model demanded all the three stake holders to equally contribute towards the capital investment and in turn equal share in profits as well as in losses. Many of the workers were not ready to take the responsibilities and risks that would come along with the ownership. After several rounds of discussions, most of the workers agreed to this new venture and few decided to quit. Since all the investment was already made by Janapada Seva Trust over the years, it was decided to pay back the two-third of the capital investment by the coordinator and workers together. Janapada Seva Trust with the spirit of trusteeship allowed the coordinator and workers to take their share of two third profits obtained from the Khadi activity with the condition of reinvesting back towards their share of capital investment. Accordingly, all the required investments were made in the next ten months by the coordinator and workers to become equal owners of the enterprise.

As a next step, a set of guidelines for the enterprise were developed through a detailed discussions with all the concerned stake holders. It was decided that a minimum of 20 hours of work per week in the enterprise as the eligibility criteria to become an investor. By doing so, it stood contrary to the prevailing investment mechanism that allows anyone having required capital to invest and make profits without active participation in that particular enterprise. Further, passbooks were designed along with the guidelines printed. These passbooks are given to everyone who is part of the enterprise. Monthly expenditure and revenue generated are disclosed in the monthly meetings and those figures are entered on everyone's passbooks. This financial transparency has brought more trust within the enterprise. As suggested in the previous chapter, the guidelines of the enterprise advocate decision making based on consensus. By doing so, it has been ensured that everyone's voice is heard in the decision making process irrespective of their social positions. However, the degree of participation in the process varies from person to person because of their distinct personalities, upbringing and social conditioning.

This three stake holder model has ensured more control for workers over their lives. According to Pushpa, a weaver,

> I worked for a year in a garment factory earlier. I know how things work in other places. But it is different here. We have more freedom than in the factory. If there is anything wrong in the workplace, we can ask in front of everyone at the daily prayer meeting.

Similarly, Savitha, another weaver, claims,

> I like the work for multiple reasons. There is no need for any educational qualification to work here. We work together as a collective and are encouraged to take up ownership of the activity. I get to learn new things and meet new people. The campus is nice

and, if we want, we can bring our children along with us. In every sense, the place is cooperative like a home.

Although the guidelines of the enterprise allow majoritarian decision making if failed to reach agreement in consecutive three attempts, all the decisions so far have been made based on consensus. The key reason for this success is the scale of the enterprise. As suggested in the previous chapter, a conscious decision has been made to not to scale the enterprise beyond 50 people to ensure democratic atmosphere conducive for reaching consensus. It is evident that reaching agreement beyond this optimum scale becomes more difficult and the system demands hierarchy to manage. This optimum scale of the organisation has also promoted a more efficient operation of production activities because it enables better coordination among the workers. Here the idea of growth is horizontal than vertical. The intention is to encourage similar enterprises to emerge at different places rather than monopolising the sector by one single entity. Therefore, horizontal conception of growth becomes essential if the focus is to improve the personality of people involved.

Profits are distributed amongst its members once every four months, with 25% of the profits retained by the enterprise as a reserve fund. To ensure social security of individuals who are part of Janapada Khadi, various funds have been created. Five percent of workers' monthly salary along with an equal contribution from the reserve fund is kept aside as pension fund. Two percent of the profits is kept aside as a health fund, which can be utilised by the members for any medical emergencies. Another 2% is allocated towards providing bonus for members who are ineligible to make an investment such as persons above 60 years of age and individuals who work less than 20 hours a week.

Another fund has been created out of profits, referred to as the 'God's aid,' exemplifies the trust and solidarity which the members share. One percent of the profit is kept towards this aid in a box, which can be accessed by all the members of the institution for any emergency need. Members neither require permission from others nor do they have to disclose to other members their intention or purpose of accessing the money from this fund. Any money thus taken is expected to be returned within a month, with a nominal additional amount if possible. For the members, the responsibility of using the fund and its accountability are owed to God and to each other. Initially when this fund started with Rs 1,000 ($12), there were a lot of speculations that somebody will take all the money. However, as a contrary, the amount had gone up to Rs 1,120 ($13.4) by the end of one year. Now the God's aid has the funds of about Rs 10,000 ($128). The existence of this fund and its working serves, perhaps, as a testimony for the mutual trust, respect and support workers provide each other during moments of personal crisis. A further 10% of the profit is utilised for community development programmes discussed under the the previous section on morality and the remaining 60% is shared among members according to their investment share.

Economy

The living wages for workers have been decided collectively and a fixed income differential of 3:1 is in place between the highest paid and the lowest paid worker to limit the income inequality within the organisation. The activities of Janapada Khadi involve weaving, natural dyeing and marketing. The sizing is carried out by weavers themselves and paid Rs 1 ($0.01) per hank. One person makes the warp and in the spare time she does weaving. No one gets the fixed salary. Everyone's income is connected to production and marketing. So, everybody has to discharge their duties and work together to earn their bread. This has ensured minimum required efficiency within the enterprise. The average earning of the warper cum weaver varies between Rs 7,000 ($88) to Rs 9,000 ($114) per month. The bobbin winding is carried out in the homes of the workers as a part-time occupation, mainly by elderly employees. They are paid Rs 2 ($0.02) per hank, and on average they earn about Rs 2,000 ($25) to Rs 3,000 ($38) per month. The pirn winding and weaving are carried out by weavers, who are paid about Rs 50 ($0.63) to 60 ($0.76) per meter and earn around Rs 6,000 ($76) to Rs 9,000 ($114) per month. Further, a differential rate has been fixed for weaving. If a weaver produces more than 75 meters per month, then gets Rs 60 ($0.76) per meter of production. If the production is less than 75 meters in a month, then gets Rs 50 ($0.63) per meter of production. This differential rate has ensured the minimum breakeven production. The income of the workers, particularly the weavers, is twice the income of weavers of other Khadi institutions. The natural dyeing is carried out according to the demand of the weaving unit. The rest of the time, dyers partici-pate in other production and sales-related activities. The dyers are paid Rs 294 ($3.72) per kg of yarn or fabric dyeing and earn about Rs 6,000 ($76) to Rs 9,000 ($114) per month. The income of the coordinator is linked to the total production and sales of the Khadi institution and earns about Rs 5,000 ($63) to Rs 10,000 ($126) per month. Apart from the monthly income, each worker obtains a profit share of about Rs 6,000 ($76) to Rs 8,000 ($101) in an average once in four months. Further, 5% wage hike is made mandatory every year if the enterprise stands on annual profits.

A self-help group has also been created. According to Harini, a young weaver,

> As you know, it is not that easy to get loans at a low interest rate. However, the bank gives money to self-help groups, often without interest. Recently, I borrowed money from our self-help group to make some investment in our Khadi activity.

Sushma, a colleague of Harini's, recounts, 'Last year, my daughter got married. Without the support of our self-help group, it would have been difficult for me to mobilise funds for her marriage.' These statements show that self-help group has significantly enhanced the financial security.

Work atmosphere at Janapada Khadi is quite in contrast to other Khadi institutions. Workers have greater flexibility in their work hours with more time for socialising. Full-time workers, such as warper and weavers, start the work around 9 am, after finishing their household responsibilities. They all assemble every day at 11 am for a prayer meeting, where prayers are sung and work concerns are raised, if any. The meeting also acts as a space for interaction with frequent visitors. The workers bring food from their homes and lunch together during their break. They leave the workplace around 5 pm.

Since the unit is small, there are no floor managers, where individuals are guided by a clearer understanding of their roles and responsibilities. To some extent, there is recognition among workers of the importance of balancing both physical and intellectual work to improve their personality. As a result, a maximum limit of 150 meters per month per weaver has been fixed on production. Since individuals are not allowed to produce more than the set limit, employees have more control over their work lives; they are able to plan their work hours and escape the trap of unceasing and unthinking production. This has enabled them to participate in other community development activities like group reading, watching films, theatre productions, potluck meals, field visits, games and so on. This maximum limit on production stands contrary to the prevailing system that demands minimum production on hourly basis resulting in regimented work condition.

The perceptions of people involved at Janapada Khadi are slightly different from that of other people employed in other Khadi institutions. Most of the workers at the institution have a favourable opinion on their work. Pushpa, one of the weavers, states, 'I enjoy working here because there is no work pressure, and I earn a fairly good remuneration for my work.' Even though the same opinion is held by many of

Pushpa's co-workers, the perspective is different among bobbin winders. Narasimha, a 70-year-old bobbin winder, states, 'On the one hand, I am happy that I can work from home. On the other, I am unhappy because of the inconsistent quality of yarn, low wages and irregular work.' Even though most of the workers are pleased with their income, there is a desire to earn more. Many of them, particularly weavers and dyers, are content with their children continuing in the same occupation, though a majority of them aspire to see them in occupations that entail less physical labour. Ragini, a weaver, says, 'My children should do easier work. They should get a job according to their education.' Savitha, her co-worker, expresses, 'I would like my daughter to be a teacher.'

There is a basic understanding of the broader implications of their work on the environment and society. For example, Prakash, a natural dyer, states, 'We use only natural dyes because they do not pollute the water. As you see here, the used water in the process directly goes to the banana plantation and is not at all harmful.' They know where their raw materials come from and where the finished Khadi products are sold. According to Manju, a weaver, 'We get yarn from another Khadi institution near Mysuru. Last year, we had gone there to meet and interact with the spinners. Their life is more difficult than ours.' They also have a broad understanding of Khadi ideology and its history. 'The objective of Khadi is to provide employment to people' says Sowmya, who works as a saleswoman. Similarly, Ragini, a weaver states, 'Khadi is connected to the freedom movement. We have seen that in a film that was screened to us a few years ago. I do not remember the name, but an English actor had beautifully played Gandhi's character.'

Workers are often motivated to participate in Khadi promotions. This has encouraged the self-consumption of Khadi among its producers. According to Savitha, a weaver,

I have bought a saree that was woven by me after seeing pictures of myself wearing it as part of a photoshoot. Until then, I had not imagined that it would look so nice on me. I had thought that it was only for urban people. Now I wear it once in a while during festivals or at events organised at the institution.

The self-consumption of Khadi by producers themselves is the direct result of their steady living income over the years. A rigorous marketing system has ensured the flow of capital and in turn purchasing power back to the hands of rural producers from urban centres. The Khadi materials produced are sold mainly in the form of fabrics as well as unstitched garments such as sarees, towels, stoles, lungis, handkerchiefs, etc. The 50% of the marketing is done through the channel of business to business. For example, there are collaborations with Tula,[c] a non-profit social enterprise that aims to restore equilibrium in the cotton value chain and Kandu,[d] a brown cotton initiative that aims to build a fair and sustainable cotton value chain. These collaborations have been longstanding because of the prompt fulfilment of orders and payments. Similar collaborations are also being constantly explored with different kinds of institutions, like schools and companies, to encourage regular purchases. Such collaborations help to better market products and reduce sales pressure. Apart from this, business-to-consumer channel is also used to market the produces though a physical store, exhibitions and e-commerce platform.

A conscious consumer base who understands the positive implication of Khadi on environment and society have been built though regular social media engagements. For example, Niveditha, a 32-year-old regular customer says,

> I had never liked wearing Khadi before because I had presumed that it is not modern enough. But after years of exposure to the ground reality, I have realised that Khadi is the way to attain sustainable and equitable world. Since then, Khadi has been my preference.

Further, our customers are constantly encouraged to visit the enterprise. Seeing and experiencing the production process can have a significant positive impact on a consumers' perspective and their moral consciousness. For example, Emily, an English customer, expressed the following after her visit to the production centre:

> I knew very little about Khadi before coming here. I do yoga and heard that Khadi is sustainable. I feel oddly energised, but it is true. I feel it is very exciting to see what they are doing. Creating community and empowering people, I think it is quite beautiful. Not allowing overproduction, keeping it small and keeping it sustainable. I am very much a fabric person. The colours are nice, and block printing would be a good idea. Since I have seen the production, I definitely feel a connection with the material that I am purchasing. Certainly, knowing its history would make me want to buy more.

Further, these direct interactions with consumers have also enhanced the self-respect of the workers. For example, Prakash, a dyer states that

'I like working here because I get a chance to meet visitors from across the world and tell them about my work.' Although, Janapada Khadi is not perfect, it is drawing the necessary public attention[1] and I believe that with all the efforts that have been made so far has moved it closer to what Gandhi calls 'a miniature swaraj.'[2[p.285]])

Notes

a More about Janapada Khadi initiative can be found at https://janapadakhadi.com.
b More about Janapada Seva Trust can be found at http://www.janapada.org.
c More about Tula initiative can be found at http://tula.org.in.
d More about Kandu can be found at https://kandu.in.

References

1 Suvarna P. Weaving together equity and well-being. *Deccan Herald*. 2022 May 22.
2 Gandhi MK. Miniature swaraj. *Young India*. 1925 Aug 20.

Final remarks

In this book, I have tried to present and defend the swaraj development paradigm as a way to establish a sustainable and equitable world. I have discussed the swaraj development approach, a distinct three-pronged method to understand social order and its transformation. A comprehensive swaraj development theory has been constructed based on the writings of Gandhi and Kumarappa. Further, I have demonstrated the method of translating this theory into practice by using the distinct three-pronged approach of the swaraj development paradigm. The case study of the khadi sector has provided valuable insights on challenges that may arise as we try to embrace swaraj development paradigm. The search for pragmatic steps to overcome those challenges has shown the possible means to establish swaraj within the khadi sector. Importantly, the practicability of many of these suggested pragmatic steps has been demonstrated through the Janapada Khadi initiative. Although the case study of khadi sector is a small constituent of the larger development scheme, still we could derive pointers to make swaraj development vision a reality. Today, all over the world, most of the nation-states are striving to attain the glorious final stage of high mass consumption society as proposed by American economist Walt Whitman Rostow through the mantra of economic growth under the disguise of sustainable development. This has made the morality of maximising own pleasure, political centralisation, and efficiency driven economy as key forces shaping the living condition across the globe similar to the case of khadi sector. Therefore, the khadi case study provides many important universally applicable insights that help to strengthen the morality of the greatest good of all among the masses, bring decentralisation in power relations, and enhance self-sufficiency in material relations. In short, this book is my attempt to provide a blueprint of the Swaraj Development Paradigm that could be adopted by individuals, communities, and nation-states to attain a non-violent global social order and in turn world peace.

Index

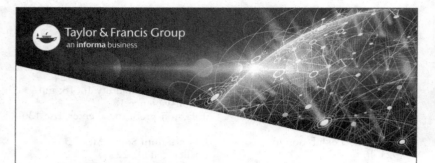

Printed in the United States
by Baker & Taylor Publisher Services

Printed in the United States
by Baker & Taylor Publisher Services